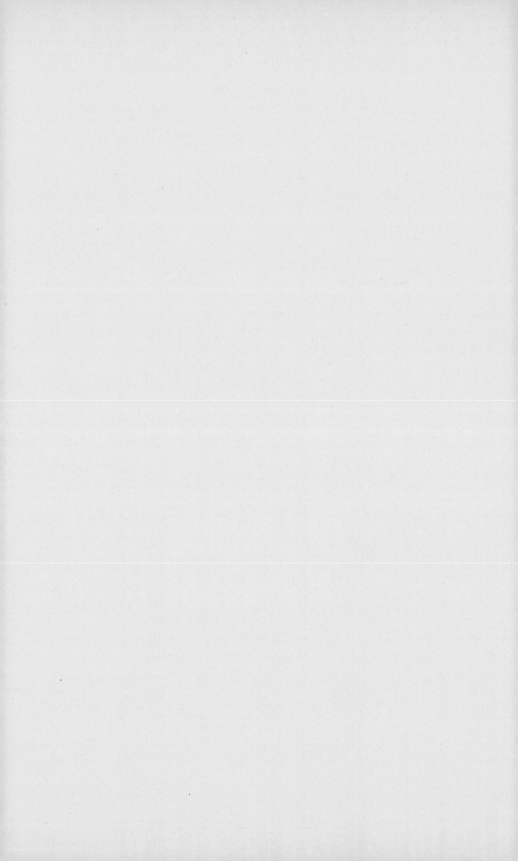

China Versus the West

China Versus the West

The Global Power Shift of the 21st Century

Ivan Tselichtchev

WILEY

John Wiley & Sons Singapore Pte. Ltd.

Other Wiley Editorial Offices
John Wiley & Sons, 111 River Street, Hoboken, NJ 07030, USA
John Wiley & Sons, The Atrium, Southern Gate, Chichester, West Sussex, P019 8SQ, United Kingdom
John Wiley & Sons (Canada) Ltd., 5353 Dundas Street West, Suite 400, Toronto, Ontario, M9B 6HB, Canada
John Wiley & Sons Australia Ltd., 42 McDougall Street, Milton, Queensland 4064, Australia
Wiley-VCH, Boschstrasse 12, D-69469 Weinheim, Germany

Library of Congress Cataloging-in-Publication Data

ISBN 978-0-470-82972-1 (Hardback)
ISBN 978-0-470-82974-5 (ePDF)
ISBN 978-0-470-82973-8 (Mobi)
ISBN 978-0-470-82975-2 (ePub)

Typeset in 11.5/14pt BemboAR-Roman by MPS Limited, a Macmillan Company, Chennai, India

Printed in Singapore by Markono Print Media

10 9 8 7 6 5 4 3 2 1

To Maxim and Olga

Contents

Foreword

My good friend Ivan Tselichtchev is an internationally renowned economist and scholar who enjoys great respect and a good reputation as a researcher, especially in the area of world economics and business. The author of the masterpiece *Asia's Turning Point*, Tselichtchev has taken a new step with *China versus the West*, a book presenting a comprehensive and accurate look at the subtle changes in the balance of power between emerging economies like China and the developed Western economies of the United States, Europe, and Japan.

In this new multilevel competitive world, global economic growth is driven by the emerging entities, rather than Western economies.

Through Tselichtchev's precise analysis, the reader sees the areas in which China has been leading the world or catching up with the developed states, as well as the areas where the traditional West still maintains its advantage and is likely to further strengthen its position. Along with articulating many valuable suggestions and ideas, Tselichtchev vividly shows how wise government policies and business strategies are needed to address the fundamental changes in the global economic environment. He articulates a unique series of proposals to and options for Western business communities on how to deal with China's emergence as a leading manufacturer and exporter.

This book offers systematic, unique, incisive, and thought-provoking analysis of the various factors that led to the global economic crisis of 2008–2009 and provides a deep insight into the impact of the crisis on the balance of economic power between China and the West, with their different institutional structures. Tselichtchev finds strong arguments to vividly illustrate how the structural dimension of the Western economic crisis dramatically shifted the balance of power in China's favor, vividly showing that China proved to be stronger both structurally and macroeconomically than most Western countries. This helps readers to rethink the essence of the Chinese model and define it in a new way. The author also brings to light China's problems, weaknesses, and prospects for political development.

Tselichtchev's book provides a very human and in-depth analysis and discussion of the complex issues as he shares his Chinese impressions and experiences, and summarizes the trends and changes in the Western economies impacted by their business relations with China. The author provides unique suggestions and convincing arguments from different perspectives, addressing the key issues. He shows the uniqueness of China's role in the global economic history and the essence of its status in today's multipolar global system where no country alone can "dominate the world." From now on, a vigorous and open China is creating a historic opportunity for the West.

For all those who want to learn more about the current economic developments and economic structures of China and the West, and about the world economy as a whole, as well for those who are searching for their place and role in this world, this book is a must. In particular, it is a valuable resource for policy makers, businesspeople, and experts and scholars in the economic fields, as well as for educational institutions and for mass media people.

Ivan Tselichtchev's extensive international experience, combined with his great writing ability, makes for a spectacular read.

Yang Yongxin
楊永新

Senior Advisor, China Chemical Energy Saving Committee

Council Member, Shanghai Economic Management Consulting Association

Executive Director, China Hao Hua Plastics City

Chairman, Haobo International Logistics Management Committee, Shanghai

Preface

C hina's emergence as a new superpower and an undisputed economic leader of the non-Western world is one of the most important global developments of the early twenty-first century.

There are many books and articles on China's rise. Their authors have vividly shown its remarkable scale and breathtaking speed. In this regard, perhaps, there is nothing left to argue about.

Our book is not about China's rise. We will not even use the term.

It is time to make a step forward. The purpose of this book is to present a comprehensive picture of the economic power balance between China and the West in today's world, to show how and why it has been changing over time, especially since the beginning of the new century, and, where possible, to articulate the directions of change expected in this decade and beyond.

Both China and the West are our main heroes. Other heroes, especially a cohort of large emerging market countries starting from India, are also present.

The term *West* is not geographical: It includes all old industrially developed economies: North America, Western Europe, Japan, Australia, and New Zealand (the new industrially developed economies are four

Asian tigers: Singapore, Hong Kong, South Korea, and Taiwan). In this book, due to inevitable space constraints, the Western part of the analysis is concentrated mostly on the United States, Japan, Germany, France, the United Kingdom, and Italy.

In Part One we explore the West-China balance of power in manufacturing production, merchandise trade, commercial services, and finance. There is an endless torrent of information about China's rushing ahead and occupying top positions in one sector of the global economy after another. Our aim is to let readers clearly see in what particular areas and product segments China has increased its power significantly and is now leading, in what areas and segments it is rapidly catching up, and the areas where, in spite of China's progress, the West retains superiority and has a chance to enhance it further.

In particular, we explore how China widens the scope of its merchandise export offensive and what options this offensive leaves for Western manufacturers.

We argue that the West, both businesses and governments, is not doing enough to take advantage of the business opportunities provided by China's growth, especially regarding China-bound exports of both goods and services. A big battle for the Chinese market is just starting, and the Western side has to move fast not to be left out.

The global economic and financial crisis of 2008–2009 exerted enormous influence on the balance of power in the world economy, making China, in relative terms, much stronger and weakening the West. This is the major theme of Part Two. We argue that the crisis was not global but Western, and manifested a failure (though, of course, not the end) of the Western, first of all the American (or Anglo-Saxon) model of capitalism. We define the major dimensions and reasons for the failure, the latter starting from unsustainable consumption patterns and ending with the inability to contain potentially disruptive financial transactions. In our view, the problem was also Western capitalism's moral failure.

Now that the crisis is over, major Western economies are changing a lot to address the issues it posed. Yet, unfortunately, they will be suffering from the crisis aftershocks for years to come—exacerbating public debts and worsening employment conditions being a clear warning. The point we are making is that the crisis resulted from the structural weaknesses of Western capitalism, while China's resilience was rooted in its structural strength, which is now providing a springboard for further growth.

This assumption naturally brings us to investigate the Chinese model of capitalism and to compare it with the Western one in broader terms. We propose a new definition of Chinese capitalism. In our view, it is not Western capitalism's opposite. We trace its evolution toward more markets, competition, and freedom for enterprises, state-owned companies included. On the other hand, we argue that the Chinese state not only actively supports domestic enterprises and industries, but also plays the role of a demanding company owner and a tough supervisor, resolutely containing financial risks.

Can China lead global growth in the 2010s through the expansion of its domestic market, in line with a currently popular concept of global rebalancing? This is one more hot issue to be discussed in depth.

Part Three looks at five major areas where the West's and China's economic interests clash: trade and the exchange rate of the yuan, environment, natural resources, technologies, and company acquisitions. Tracing and analyzing the major developments, we arrive at the conclusion that in most of those areas China is on the offensive and that more often than not it succeeds in making things change in the directions it wants them to. We try to explain the reasons and to explore various options for the West's response.

In short, in this book we try to diagnose the West-China economic power shift, answering the four key questions: In what areas? How big and how fast? Why? and What to do?

We also kindly ask the reader not to skip the "Epilogue: China, the West, and the World" where we discuss the global context and global implications of the West-China economic power shift and articulate a number of key conclusions. We show why, in spite of its dramatic rise, China will not become a world ruler and there will be no new Pax Sinica.

We did our best to make the book lively and reader-friendly, selecting really interesting and important facts and storylines. It contains many specific examples, which, we hope, will make it easier to understand and to feel both Western and Chinese realities. Some of them reflect our own on-the-spot experiences. We have also added to it a little bit of Japanese flavor, because Japan is the country where we have been living for more than 20 years and a very good and relevant place to research many of the issues we raise.

We hope that *China versus the West* will be useful and pleasant reading for everyone seeking to understand the major global developments of our time, including businesspeople and policy makers, scholars, analysts and journalists, professors, and university or business school students.

Acknowledgments

This book will see the world thanks to cooperation and support from many colleagues and friends.

Frank-Jurgen Richter, chairman of Horasis and the host of Global China Business Meetings, provided valuable intellectual input and much assistance in my research in Europe, offering a wonderful opportunity to participate in Horasis projects.

In Asia, I am always happy to work at INSEAD, Singapore. I am grateful to Professors Hellmut Schutte and Michael Witt, as well as the Tanoto Library staff who provided such opportunities.

Here in Japan, I am especially grateful to Mr. Shin'ichi Suzuki, president of the Ad Post Company, and a person with remarkable experience in regard to working in China, for supporting and encouraging my research and writing activities and providing invaluable advice.

Ken'ichi Imai, a Senior Fellow Emeritus of the Stanford University and Professor Emeritus of the Hitotsubashi University, has been one of the most important economists in Japan and beyond, since the start of my modest career. His writings and all our discussions provided a unique intellectual stimulus.

I'd like to say thank you to the Chuo University and especially to Professor Kenji Takita for inviting me to take part in research projects and international conferences on Asia that helped to solidify the concept of this book.

Many thanks for sharing thoughts and encouraging me to write on Asian and global issues to my old friend Hideaki Yamakawa, currently professor at the Kanazawa Gakuin University.

I always learn from Mr. Keisuke Uemura, president of the ITAC company, the R&D arm of Nagata Seiki, a leading player among Japanese producers and developers of new materials.

I am grateful to many other Japanese colleagues and friends in Tokyo, Niigata, and beyond who shared their views and encouraged my research effort.

A very important person for me, be it in Japan, Belgium, or anywhere else, is Philippe Debroux, professor at the Soka University and my co-author for my previous book, *Asia's Turning Point*. He is a wise man with deep knowledge, rich professional experience, and a beautiful sense of humor. Some parts of the book were written under the impetus of our lively discussions.

I value all the contacts, discussions, and debates I have had with Chinese scholars, businesspeople, managers of state-owned companies, journalists, and politicians I met during my China trips, here in Japan, and at the Global China Business Meetings and other international gatherings.

Thank-you, Yang Yongxin—a major manager in Shanghai, the largest industrial center in the world.

Thank-you, my friend, Yuan Pei Zhe.

And now, back to Russia—with love. Special thanks to Alexander Drozdov, the director of the Eltzin Fund and a very good journalist, for showing strong interest in my research concepts and plans, sharing his ideas, and encouraging my international research activities.

Wherever I am, I will be an "IMEMO man." IMEMO is the Russian abbreviation for the Institute of World Economy and Economic Relations of the Russian Academy of Sciences, where I started my career as a researcher.

I am grateful to academician Evgeny Primakov, the prime minister of Russia in the late 1990s, who played a very important role in setting the direction for my professional activities in the mid-1980s, when they were still at an early stage.

Thank you, my old colleagues and friends: director Alexander Dynkin, Vyacheslav Amirov, and Sergey Chughrov, who is now the editor-in-chief of *Political Studies* magazine in Moscow. Gratitude and special tribute also go to the late Vladlen Martynov and Yakov Pevzner. Apologies to many other colleagues and friends whose names cannot be mentioned due to space constraints.

Finally, last but not least, I thank my son Maxim Tselichtchev, for providing assorted kinds of technical and information support.

Introduction

Globalization has entered a critical stage, as the ongoing economic disruptions have prompted many of us to reexamine its promises. The world today is characterized by pronounced fragility and heightened uncertainty, fed by external shocks and multiple crises that are dangerously reinforcing. Against the backdrop of these unprecedented challenges we are witnessing an economic and geopolitical power shift from the developed to the emerging world.

By 2030, most of the world's largest economies will be non-Western and more than half of the world's 1,000 largest corporations will have their origins in the emerging countries. This will directly impact the way globalization works. As emerging economies rewrite the rules of globalization, the West is overtly advocating more protectionism.

One of the main criticisms made of globalization by its detractors has been that it is Western-driven and Western-centric—in other words, that the West calls the shots and that most benefits go to Western players. Yet, as globalization was gathering momentum, it assumed new and striking features that ran contrary to that Western-focused characterization.

Non-Western players started to emerge as vital sources of energy and initiative in globalization; they have become its new engines, and their companies are strengthening their global positions at an unprecedented pace.

China is the leader of the emerging world.

In the year 2010, its share of the global manufacturing exports reached 13.7 percent, up from 12.1 percent in 2009. The trend is likely to persist in this decade. Eventually, China will reach a point at which mounting labor costs trigger declining shares in low-end exports, offsetting gains in the mid and high-end value segments. But we are not there yet. China's goods are more high-end than before, but it is still predominantly a labor-intensive, low-end export power, excelling in production of commodities such as clothing, textiles, footwear, and toys.

However, the future of exports from China will be led by equipment manufacturers, and, although they may not be penetrating Western markets, competition in third markets is intensifying. The greatest shock that might face European and U.S. manufacturers is the full-scale export of Chinese manufacturing capability similar to that of the Japanese entry into the U.S. and European markets several decades ago.

China wishes to establish its global image as that of a benign power in many sectors, but it will not be perceived as mature if it doles out money to spent causes. It bought into the U.S. debt, perhaps fueling too much credit and inflaming U.S. purchase of cheap Chinese-made goods. It will have learned that hard lesson, and now Europe has to behave in a more relevant way than the old United States did in order to be creditworthy in China's eyes. That seems fair.

China versus the West—a new book by Ivan Tselichtchev, a leading expert, scholar, and writer on international economy, business, and politics—is very timely and unique. It is an innovative book, innovative for several reasons.

First, the author has found his unique angle. The book provides a deep insight into this new globalization stage I mentioned at the beginning, vividly depicting its major characteristics. Its focus is the economic power balance between China, a new emerging market superpower, and the developed West, and the way this balance is changing. It is essentially the first book presenting a comprehensive picture of the economic power balance between the two, based on the analysis of a remarkably wide range of carefully selected data. The author avoids simplified assumptions about China's rise and the West's fall (perhaps this topic is already somewhat overdone), analyzing the issues in all their complexity and presenting conclusions resulting from thorough research.

Starting from an in-depth analysis of the power balance in particular fields—manufacturing production, merchandise exports, services, and finance—Tselichtchev moves on to investigate tectonic changes in the global arena, spurred by the financial and economic crisis of 2008 and 2009. His crucial point is that in the wake of the crisis and in its aftermath China has proved to be structurally and macroeconomically stronger that most Western countries. This brings him to a new definition of the Chinese model of capitalism per se. Finally, he puts together a series of exciting stories about the China-West rivalry ("economic wars") in particular fields: trade/currency, environment, natural resources, technologies, and company acquisitions.

Second, the book resolutely rises against stereotypes and clichés, making us reconsider many key assumptions. Indeed, China is already not only a world factory, but also a world research lab and a leader in green business. There is a lot of talk about the Chinese economy's overheating and asset bubble risks, but it is exactly China that has been most successful in containing the bubble already for three decades of uninterrupted growth, and exactly the West that was incapable of stopping devastating waves of financial speculation. China's long-term uninterrupted growth itself is a unique phenomenon in the history of market economies, and has to be properly assessed and explained. There are concerns about China's facing a threat of political turmoil stemming from the people's impatience with the one-party rule, or social turmoil due to expanding income gaps. However, though critical of many aspects of China's domestic and foreign policy, the author argues that apparently there is still a lot of room for further political evolution within the framework of the one-party dominance, and that income gaps in China are of a less socially explosive character because low-income families' incomes and living standards are also rising fast.

Third, the book contains many valuable proposals and ideas both for policy makers and for businesspeople. For instance, it presents in a systematic way strategic options for Western manufacturers in the wake of China's production/export offensive and proposes scenarios for West-China interaction on global environmental issues. Being imaginative, the author avoids building castles made of sand. He is searching for solutions that are feasible and realistic.

Fourth, it is a book written in a unique genre. There is a lot of valuable and thorough academic research. However, it is presented as an informal conversation with the reader, in language easy to understand for a very wide audience; it may often be perceived almost like a novel with its own drama and a breathtaking plot. It is full of passion and emotional power almost unexpected from a book on the economy and business. It conveys the spirit of our time, its nerve, its complexity, its conflicts, and sometimes even its tragedy. Still, you will also have moments of intellectual relaxation while reading several passages sparkling with charming humor.

After all, the book ends on an optimistic note. There should be "more China" in our (Westerners') lives, so that more and more of us could discover their "China opportunity."

Enjoy reading.

Frank-Jürgen Richter

Chairman, Horasis — The Global Visions Community
Host of Global China Business Meetings,
Global India Business Meetings,
Global Russia Business Meetings, and
Global Arab Business Meetings (www.horasis.org)

Part One

CHINA AS THE WORLD'S LEADING PRODUCING, EXPORTING, AND FINANCIAL POWER: TO WHAT EXTENT, WHERE, AND WHY?

A t the start of the second decade of the twenty-first century, the picture looks like this: Manufacturing industries where China is not leading the world in production volumes have become an exception. China is an undisputed leader in export volumes of electrical/ electronic products and light industry goods. Its presence in other merchandise export markets is much smaller. Having joined the ranks of important exporters of services, it still remains far behind the United States and other leading services nations—services are not its strong point. The Chinese state is emerging as effectively the world's number one financial powerhouse (soon you will feel it stronger, as Beijing will become a key emergency lender for cash-strapped Western governments), but China's private investors are still relatively weak and financial assets of its households are meager.

1

Chapter 1

GDP: Toward the U.S.-China Duopoly

J ust 10 years ago, in 2001, China's nominal Gross Domestic Product (GDP) was the sixth-largest in the world: only a little larger than Italy's. It comprised 12.9 percent of the GDP of the United States and 32.4 percent of Japan. By 2010, when China overtook Japan to become the second-largest economy in the world, it reached 41.2 percent and 107.7 percent respectively, exceeding Germany's GDP by 78.8 percent, Britain's 2.6 times, France's 2.3 times, and Italy's 2.9 times (Table 1.1).

Within the same period, the United States' share of the global GDP dropped from 32.1 percent to 23.1 percent, while that of China surged from 4.1 percent to 9.3 percent (IMF 2011).

Between 2001 and 2010, China's GDP in current dollars increased 4.4 times against 1.4 times in the United States, 1.9 times in France, 1.8 times in Italy, 1.7 times in Germany, and 1.5 times in the United Kingdom. In India it rose 3.4 times, in South Korea twice.

Table 1.1   GDP at Current Prices ($ billion)

	2001	2010
United States	10,286	14,527
China	1,325	5,878
Japan	4,095	5,459
Germany	1,892	3,286
United Kingdom	1,471	2,250
France	1,341	2,563
Italy	1,118	2,055
India	488	1,632
World	32,008	62,911

SOURCE: IMF WEO Database, September 2011.

Our simple simulation has shown that, if in this decade the U.S. annual nominal GDP growth averages 3 percent and China's (in current dollars) 10 percent,[1] in 2020 the size of the Chinese economy will reach three-quarters that of the United States. (According to the IMF forecast, in 2016 China's GDP will be about 60 percent that of the United States and 170 percent of Japan's.)

It looks most probable that at the end of this decade, in terms of the size of the economy, China and the United States will be the two giants towering high above all other countries and that China will catch up with America somewhere in the middle of the 2020s. As far as the size of national economies is concerned, the global economy is rapidly moving toward a duopolistic structure with the United States and China somewhat resembling the two Petronas Towers in Kuala Lumpur, Malaysia, whose height by far exceeds that of any other building in the city.

One more country looked upon as a new great economic power comparable to China is India. This conventional view is wrong, at least at this point. No doubt, as the second-largest emerging economy, India is becoming increasingly important, but compared to China, it is in a different weight category, and the global impact of its growth is much smaller.[2]

In 2001, India's current GDP equaled 36.8 percent of the Chinese, and in 2010 the proportion fell to just 27.8 percent. In other words, today the Chinese economy is almost four times as large as the Indian, and the gap is widening because China is growing faster.

GDP comparisons based on the national currencies' exchange rates, may not reflect China's real economic strength versus the United States (and the West in general), because Chinese prices are much lower. In other words, for one and the same product or service in China you have to pay less dollars than in the United States. In this regard, the estimate based on the currencies' purchasing power parities is more accurate. Calculated on the PPP basis, in 2010 China's GDP was already 69.7 percent that of the United States and 2.3 times larger than the GDP of Japan.

As for the real GDP, in China its average growth rate for 2001–2010 was 10.5 percent as opposed to 1.7 percent in the United States, 1.4 percent in the United Kingdom, 1.2 percent in France, 0.9 percent in Germany, and 0.7 percent in Japan (Table 1.2). In India it was 7.6 percent. (Roughly, an annual 7 percent growth rate will double the GDP within 10 years.)

In the 2000s, China's (and, to a lesser extent, India's) growth was steadily accelerating and reached its peak in 2007. Then, though having fallen by several percentage points, it remained comfortably

Table 1.2   Real GDP Growth Rates in 2000–2010 (%)

	2001	2002	2003	2004	2005	2006	2007	2008	2009	2010
China	8.3	9.1	10.0	10.1	11.3	12.7	14.2	9.6	9.2	10.3
United States	1.1	1.8	2.5	3.5	3.1	2.7	1.9	−0.3	−3.5	3.0
Japan	0.2	0.3	1.4	2.7	1.9	2.0	2.4	−1.2	−6.3	4.0
Germany	1.4	0.0	−0.4	0.7	0.8	3.9	3.4	0.8	−5.1	3.6
France	1.8	0.9	0.9	2.3	1.9	2.7	2.2	−0.2	−2.6	1.4
UK	2.5	2.1	2.8	3.0	2.2	2.8	2.7	−0.1	−4.9	1.4
Italy	1.8	0.5	−0.0	1.5	0.7	2.0	1.5	−1.3	−5.2	1.3
India	3.9	4.6	6.9	7.5	9.0	9.5	10.0	6.2	6.8	10.1

SOURCE: IMF WEO Database, September 2011.

positive in 2008–2009. Major Western economies grew reasonably well (around 2–3 percent a year) in 2004–2007, but registered a very low growth in 2001–2003 and a zero/negative growth in 2008–2009.

In 2010, China's (and India's) growth rates became double-digit, while the West entered a phase of a sluggish recovery. Only Germany is emerging as a growth engine in Europe, while, as of mid-2011, the recovery in the United States is somewhat losing momentum, and pro-growth trends in Japan have been undermined by the devastating earthquake and the nuclear disaster.

Compared to Western economies, China looks much better in terms of not only average growth rates (this may be natural as economic development stages are different), but also growth stability. Notably, since the start of China's market transition in 1978–1979 and up to the current period, it has never experienced a recession, and there is little reason to believe that one will come in the 2010s (we will return to this point later on).

Notes

1. Ten percent growth of nominal GDP means about 7 percent growth of real GDP, allowing for an inflation rate of 5 percent. Seven percent is the growth target for the period of China's twelfth Five-Year Plan (2011–2015), which, as many economists (the author included) believe, represents a bottom line. It is more than likely that in reality China will grow faster. Thus, regarding China, the assumption for this simulation is rather conservative. For the United States, a 3 percent nominal growth rate means 2.5 percent real growth if the inflation rate is 2 percent and 2.7 percent real growth if it is 1 percent.

2. Still, between 2001 and 2010, India's GDP rose from 4.7 percent to 11.2 percent of the United States, from 11.9 percent to 29.9 percent of Japan's, from 25.7 percent to 49.7 percent of Germany's, from 33.0 percent to 72.5 percent of the United Kingdom, and from 36.2 percent to 63.7 percent of France's. In 2010, it was the world's tenth-largest economy, while in 2001 it was at number 14. The countries it overtook are Spain, Canada, Mexico, and South Korea.

Chapter 2

Manufacturing Output: China Is Already the Number One

I n manufacturing output, the shift of global power balance is drastic. In this sector the West has lost its dynamics, and all the growth energy has gone to China and other emerging economies.

Between 2001 and 2009, the new economic giant increased its manufacturing output (value added in 2005 U.S. dollars) by 136.8 percent (2.368 times), while growth in the West was very slow if not negative. In all major European economies, manufacturing output in 2009 was smaller than in 2001. As 2009 was the year of the worst recession of the postwar era, we will also present the data on the Western countries' manufacturing output growth between 2001 and 2007, when it reached its precrisis peak. So, between 2001 and 2009, the manufacturing value added in the United States increased 15.9 percent (between

2001 and 2007, the increase was 20.7 percent) and in Japan 14.6 percent (24.3 percent). In Germany, it fell by 8.8 percent (the increase in the 2001–2007 period was 15.9 percent), in France 7.4 percent (an increase of 6.6 percent), in the United Kingdom 12.2 percent (an increase of 1.5 percent), and in Italy 18.0 percent (an increase of 2.0 percent). In India between 2001 and 2009, the increase was 97 percent, but its manufacturing output is less than one-tenth that of China.

As for absolute numbers, in 2008 China's manufacturing output (value added in current dollars) exceeded that of the United States: $1.87 trillion and $1.79 trillion, respectively. According to the latest available data, in 2009 its manufacturing value added hit 2.05 trillion or 21.2 percent of the world's total. The figures for the United States are 1.78 trillion and 18.4 percent, respectively. Japan's manufacturing output ($1.05 trillion) was only half that of China, and Germany's ($568 billion) a little more than one-fourth (United Nations 2010).[1]

As far as production volumes are concerned, in the first decade of the twenty-first century China emerged and consolidated its position as the world's largest, if not dominant, producer of a wide variety of manufacturing goods, often leaving all other contenders far behind. In contrast, the range of major manufacturing items whose production is led by Western countries has significantly narrowed.

If current differentials in the growth dynamics are preserved, already in the second half of this decade China's production of manufactured goods will be greater than that of the United States and Japan combined.

Besides, as in the case of GDP, comparisons based on the national currencies' exchange rates have to be treated with caution: Their results may be biased in the West's favor because one and the same product is usually cheaper in China than in the West.

Note

1. According to other sources, as of 2009, the United States was still slightly ahead, but China would certainly overtake it in the very near future. UNIDO, presenting the data on the manufacturing value added in constant 2000 U.S. dollars, ranks the United States first and China second: Their shares of the world total in 2010 were estimated at 23.3 percent and 15.4 percent, respectively (UNIDO 2011).

Chapter 3

Merchandise Exports: From China's Lead to China's Dominance?

C hina has been elevating its share of world exports at a tremendous speed, drastically changing the global trade power balance within a remarkably short time.

By 2008, it had risen to the position of the number one exporter of manufacturing products with a share of 12.7 percent of the world's total. (Manufactures account for almost 70 percent of the country's total merchandise exports.)

The following year it became the largest exporter of merchandise goods as a whole, overtaking Germany; China's share of the world's total reached 10 percent. In 2010, it moved further ahead of the followers. Also, Germany ceded the number two position to the United States.

Between 2001 and 2010, China's exports increased 5.9 times as opposed to 1.4 times for the United States, 2.2 times for Germany, 1.9 times for Japan, 1.6 times for France, 1.5 times for the United Kingdom, and 1.8 times for Italy. India's exports grew 5.0 times (WTO 2011).

In 1983, it accounted for a meager 1.2 percent of global exports against 11.2 percent for the United States, 9.2 percent for Germany (the data for 1983 are for West Germany only), 8.0 percent for Japan, and 5.2 percent for France. Until 1993 it increased its portion twofold and within the next 10 years 2.4 times (Table 3.1).

In other words, since the early 1980s China has at least doubled its share of the world's merchandise exports every 10 years. If the trend continues, at the beginning of the 2020s it may account for around one-fourth of the world's total, exporting three or more times as much as the United States, Germany, or Japan. As China's share becomes higher and higher, it may be increasingly challenging to maintain its growth pace; even so, a share of 20 percent of the world exports in the early 2020s still looks quite feasible. And even if, like today, about 55 percent of China's exports are accounted for by multinationals' subsidiaries, exports of domestic Chinese companies will still significantly exceed the total for any major Western country.

Table 3.1 Share of the World Merchandise Exports (%)

	1983	1993	2003	2010
United States	11.2	12.6	9.8	8.4
Germany	9.2	10.3	10.2	8.3
France	5.2	6.0	5.3	3.8
Italy	4.0	4.6	4.1	2.9
UK	5.0	4.9	4.1	2.7
Japan	8.0	9.9	6.4	5.1
China	1.2	2.5	5.9	10.4
India	0.5	0.6	0.8	1.4
World	100.0	100.0	100.0	100.0

SOURCE: WTO International Trade Statistics.

The data presented in Table 3.1 reveal one more important trend, or rather a reversal of the trend.

Between 1983 and 1993, the United States, Japan, and the major European powers were also enhancing their shares of global merchandise exports, albeit, compared to China, at a slower pace. However, between 1993 and 2003 their shares dropped: for major European countries only slightly, but for the United States and Japan by as much as about 3 percentage points. (In 2003, though, China was still lagging behind the leaders, its exports volume comprising only 57.8 percent that of Germany's and 60.2 percent of the United States, but already 92.2 percent of Japan.) This new trend continued into the mid and late 2000s: In 2003–2010 China's share soared again, while the shares of all major developed countries registered a decline of between 1 and 2 percentage points.

To summarize, having established itself as the world's *leading* exporter, China is steadily ascending to become the *dominant* exporter.

It is not only increasing the volume of its exports, but also significantly upgrading their contents. In 2009, the portion of machinery and transport equipment rose to 49.2 percent of its total exports against 30.2 percent in 1999, while the share of clothing decreased from 15.4 percent to 8.9 percent and of other consumer goods (personal and household goods and miscellaneous items) from 21.7 percent to 13.7 percent, respectively (WTO 2010).

While China is intensifying its export offensive, in America and Europe, amid a very slow growth of output, the numbers of both manufacturing establishments and their employees are falling.

From 2000 to 2007, the number of manufacturing establishments in the United States dropped from 354,500 to 331,100 and the number of employees from 16,464 to 13,632. On an average, employment in the manufacturing sector was decreasing 3.0 percent a year. In the United Kingdom its annual fall averaged 4.0 percent, in France 1.8 percent, in Canada 1.4 percent, and in Germany 1.0 percent (U.S. Census Bureau 2011a).

Certainly, the fall in the number of establishments and declining employment can be largely explained by growing productivity and the shift of the domestic demand toward services. This is the bright side of the coin. However, the West should not console itself with such an explanation because there is also a dark side.

This dark side becomes more visible if the world economy is viewed as a single entity. The problem is that Western-based factories are losing a larger and larger portion of global output and of the global market because they curtail production in significant numbers or close altogether, outperformed by factories based in China (including the Chinese factories of Western firms). Moreover, while losing in the production segments where they currently operate, too many of them are lacking the capability to shift to other segments where they can win or remain uncontested by the Chinese.

True, the best Western manufacturers are raising productivity and sharpening their competitive edge. However, the circle of these strong players is quite limited.

The agony of weak manufacturers exacerbates the situation at the labor market: People losing their manufacturing jobs, even if they find a job in the service sector, often have to accept lower pay, worse working conditions, and less employment stability.

Chapter 4

Where China Is Leading and Where It Is Not

owever, China does not lead in manufacturing production and exports all across the board. Also, the range of its exports lead is narrower than the range of production lead because in many industries the increments in production are absorbed by the rapidly expanding domestic market. Besides, the rise in exports is supported by a dynamic growth of the imports of production inputs: intermediate products and equipment. Depending on China's position versus other major producers and exporters, all manufacturing industries can be divided into three groups.

Group One Industries: China Is the Top Producer and the Top Exporter

This group of industries consists of two major pillars. The first one is the office and telecommunication equipment sector, along with electrical machinery. The second is a variety of light industry goods: textiles and clothing, footwear, toys and games, travel goods, furniture, travel items, and so on.

In the 2000s, these sectors' production in China increased dramatically, while in the West and other major producing nations, mainly Asian, it grew at a slow pace, stagnated, or declined. As a result, China established itself as the number one producer and exporter, often running far ahead of all followers.

Office and Telecom Equipment, Electrical Machinery

The most vivid example is the office and telecommunication equipment sector. According to the UN Standard International Trade Classification (SITC), Revision 3, it consists of the two big blocs. The first one is electronic data processing (EDP) and office equipment; the second is telecommunication and sound-recording/reproducing apparatus and equipment. EDP equipment means computers, printers, computer peripheral equipment, and software. Sound-recording and reproducing equipment includes TVs and various audio-video products.

The data about production of the four key items belonging to this sector (color TVs, video products, mobile phones, and personal computers) are presented in Table 4.1. We have also added the data on digital cameras: an important product of a similar character, though the SITC includes it in a different group.

Within the previous decade, China's position underwent a fundamental and abrupt change. At the beginning, it was just one out of the several major producers; at its end, an undisputed world leader, and in the case of personal computers a dominant producing power. Also, in 2008 it accounted for 34.7 percent of the global production of flat-screen TVs.

India rapidly expanded production of mobile phones, but its presence in the markets of four other products remained insignificant.

The shares of North America and Europe in the production of all the five items plummeted, with North America halting manufacturing of video products, PCs, and digital cameras altogether, and Europe ceasing to produce digital cameras and reducing the PC production to a negligible level.

Table 4.1 Production Volumes of Five Key Electronic Items*

	Color TVs		Video Products†		Mobile Phones		Personal Computers		Digital Cameras	
	2000	2008	2000	2008	2000	2008	2000	2008	2000	2008
World	132,210 (100.0)	200,626 (100.0)	74,670 (100,0)	101,142 (100.0)	423,150 (100.0)	1,210,140 (100.0)	128,207 (100,0)	285,086 (100.0)	15,280 (100.0)	136,080 (100.0)
China	31,990 (24.2)	84,944 (42.3)	18,250 (24.4)	67,560 (66.8)	41,000 (9.7)	637,610 (52.7)	24,669 (19.2)	277,185 (97.2)	450 (2.9)	85,640 (62.9)
North America	24,022 (18.1)	24,335 (12.0)	2,070 (2.7)	0 (0.0)	52,000 (12.3)	49,690 (4.1)	30,130 (23.5)	0 (0.0)	0 (0.0)	0 (0.0)
Europe	25,270 (19.3)	40,822 (20.3)	12,650 (16.9)	3,020 (3.0)	183,400 (43.3)	92,640 (7.7)	17,180 (13.4)	540 (0.2)	0 (0.0)	0 (0.0)
Japan	2,150 (1.6)	9,010 (4.5)	6,530 (8.7)	3,420 (3.4)	55,350 (13.1)	34,990 (2.9)	9,888 (7.7)	5,655 (2.0)	11,170 (73.1)	29,650 (21.8)
South Korea	10,820 (8.2)	6,951 (3.5)	4,850 (6.5)	1,600 (1.6)	57,500 (13.6)	155,780 (12.9)	7,370 (5.7)	1,006 (3.5)	790 (5.2)	1,770 (1.3)
Taiwan							32,660 (25.5)	700 (0.2)	1,900 (12.4)	0 (0.0)
Malaysia	13,510 (9.9)	5,554 (2.8)	14,990 (20.1)	11,662 (11.0)	4,800 (1.1)	13,550 (1.1)	2,260 (1.8)	0 (0.0)	500 (0.6)	4,780 (3.5)
India					5,000	146,970‡ (12.1)				

Volume: thousand units (%).

*Data for South Korea, Taiwan, Malaysia, and India are presented only when their share of global production is significant.

†For 2000: VTRs, DVD players and DVD recorders; for 2008: DVD players, DVD recorders, BD players, and BD recorders.

‡2005.

SOURCE: Sekai Kokusei Zue 2010–2011.

The shares of Japan and South Korea were also mostly sharply down. Taiwan and Malaysia terminated production of personal computers. In addition, Malaysia effectively lost its position as one of the major production platforms for color TVs (although it noticeably increased its role as a producer of digital cameras).

However, while reducing output of the final goods, East Asian countries drastically increased production of their parts, components, and materials, which in great part were exported to China, where final products were assembled. This was one of the major reasons why East Asia preserved the dynamism of its manufacturing industries. In North America and Europe, such structural shift was much smaller in scale.

Also, it goes without saying that China's dramatic upswing to the number one position (as both a producer and an exporter) was largely the result of the production activities of multinational companies. However, in this regard, too, East Asian, not Western multinationals took the lead.

The data on exports is presented in Table 4.2. By the end of the previous decade, China commanded 34 percent of the world exports of EDP and office equipment, and almost 30 percent of the exports of telecommunication equipment (including sound-recording and reproducing apparatus and equipment). Its shares have been rising at an enormous speed.

Table 4.2   Share (%) of World Exports by Product/Country

	EDP and Office Equipment		Telecom Equipment*	
	2000	**2009**	**2000**	**2009**
World	100.0	100.0	100.0	100.0
China	5.0	34.0	6.8	29.4
United States	15.5	8.6	11.4	7.0
EU-27	30.4	28.0	38.3	29.7
Japan	9.5	4.0	10.6	4.5
South Korea	5.3	2.4	5.5	7.7

*Includes sound-recording and reproducing apparatus and equipment.
SOURCE: WTO International Trade Statistics.

In contrast, the U.S. shares for both groups of products declined by a little less than half, and the shares of Japan by more than half. The decrease of the EU-27's share was insignificant, because it includes tariff-free trade within the European Union accounting for most of the total exports of its member countries. Still, in 2009 China exported more EDP and office equipment than 27 EU countries combined and effectively the same amount of telecom equipment.

Finally, South Korea, the largest newly developed economy, known for its strong position in both sectors, also lost more than half of its share of the global EDP and office equipment market, and increased the share of the telecom equipment market by just 2.2 percentage points while China elevated its share by 22.8 percentage points. Thus, in 2009, compared to China, it was an exporter of a different weight category, although in 2000 their shares were very close.

Such changes in the export power balance are of a tectonic character. Within one decade, they made China an eventual dominant player in the global markets.

In another important development, along with the office and telecommunication equipment sector, China established itself as the leading producer and exporter of electrical machinery (including home electric appliances). Its electrical machinery exports hit $108 billion in 2008 and $92 billion in 2009, or more than twice the exports of the United States: respectively $53 billion and $45 billion; and Japan, $47 billion and $37 billion. In other words, today China exports more electrical machinery than the United States and Japan combined.

Extra-EU exports (excluding trade between EU member countries) of electrical machinery by the EU-27 states were $93 billion and $76 billion respectively (WTO 2010).

Textiles and Apparel

The second pillar, light industry, consists of many different sectors. We will focus on the textiles and apparel sector as a representative example.

In the production of textiles, China was the only major driver of global growth in the previous decade. Between 1998–1999 and 2007–2008, it accounted for as much as 86 percent of the total increase in mill use of cotton worldwide.

In 2009, its output of filament and spun yarn reached 39.7 million tonnes, or about 70 percent of the world's total. India ran second with 5.7 million tonnes and 9 percent respectively. Other producers were far behind. Production volume in the United States was 1.9 million tonnes, Taiwan 1.5 million tonnes, South Korea 1.1 million tonnes, and the rest of the world 11.9 million tonnes (Oerlikon 2010).

The data on production of man-made fibers are presented in Table 4.3.

Between 2000 and 2009, output declined in all the major producing countries except China where it increased dramatically, and India where the rise was substantial.

The output of China's apparel industry in 2009 reached an astronomical figure of 25.4 billion pieces (ResearchInChina 2010).

This breath taking rise in the volumes and share of global production naturally drove China to the position of a leading exporter. Between 2000 and 2009, its exports of clothing tripled and exports of textiles grew 3.7 times. India increased its exports 2.2 times and 63.5 percent respectively. In the exports of textiles, the EU achieved a small increment of the volume, but its share of world exports fell. Exports of all other major players declined (see Table 4.4).

In the clothing sector, the EU increased its export volume substantially which led to a small rise in its share of the world's total. However, currently, even if we count intra-EU trade, clothing

Table 4.3 Production of Man-Made Fibers by Country

	2000	2009
World	31.1 (100.0)	44.1 (100.0)
China	6.7 (21.5)	26.3 (59.6)
India	1.9 (6.1)	2.8 (6.3)
United States	4.2 (13.5)	2.3 (5.2)
Taiwan	3.2 (10.2)	2.1 (4.8)
South Korea	2.8 (9.0)	1.4 (3.2)
Indonesia	1.4 (4.5)	1.1 (2.5)
Japan	1.5 (4.8)	0.8 (1.8)

Volume: Million Tonnes (%).
SOURCE: Oerlikon. Fiber Year 2009/2010.

Table 4.4   Major Exporters of Textiles*

	2000	2009
World	157,400 (100.0)	211,054 (100.0)
China	16,135 (10.3)	59,281 (28.1)
India	5,570 (3.5)	9,105 (4.3)
EU	56,737 (36.0)	62,223 (29.5)
EU (extra-EU only)	15,567 (9.9)	18,810 (8.9)
United States	10,952 (7.0)	9,931 (4.7)
South Korea	12,710 (8.1)	9,155 (4.3)
Taiwan	11,891 (7.6)	9,931 (4.7)

Value: $ million (%).
*Clothing exports are not included.
SOURCE: WTO International Trade Statistics.

Table 4.5   Major Exporters of Clothing

	2000	2009
World	197,570 (100.0)	315,622 (100.0)
China	36,071 (18.3)	107,261 (34.0)
India	5,260 (2.7)	11,454 (3.6)
EU	56,240 (28.5)	96,797 (30.7)
EU (extra-EU only)	12,954 (6.6)	21,682 (6.9)
United States	8,629 (4.4)	4,186 (1.3)
Indonesia	4,734 (2.4)	5,915 (1.9)
South Korea	5,027 (2.5)	1,396 (0.4)
Mexico	8,631 (4.4)	4,165 (1.3)
Bangladesh	5,067 (2.6)	10,726 (3.4)
Turkey	6,533 (3.3)	11,555 (3.7)

Value: $ million (%).
SOURCE: WTO International Trade Statistics.

exports of all its 27 member countries would be below those of China (see Table 4.5).

Also, the 2000s were marked by a noticeable rise of clothing exports from Bangladesh and Turkey, but, compared to China, they remain the exporters of a lighter weight category. Exports by the United States, South Korea, and Mexico decreased.

Foreign-Owned, Domestic Private, and State-Owned Companies as Exporters

Overall, China's exports, especially in the machinery sector, are led by foreign-affiliated companies. In 2010, they accounted for 54.6 percent of the total, down from 58.3 percent in 2005 (21 Seiki Chugoku Soken 2006, 2011), but up from 52.0 percent in 2002 (Koopman, Wang, and Wei 2009). Between 2002 and 2006, the share of wholly foreign-owned firms rose from 29.4 percent to 39.3 percent, while the share of joint ventures fell from 22.6 percent to 16.6 percent (Koopman, Wang, and Wei 2009).

According to G. Redding and M. Witt, as of the end of the previous decade, out of the top 10 China-based firms exporting high-tech products, 9 were foreign-owned: 4 Taiwanese and 5 American. The Taiwanese-owned companies were leading in terms of export value, accounting for more than half of the group's total (Redding and Witt 2009).

Among domestic exporters, private firms[1] are doing much better than state-owned enterprises (SOE) whose role in China's export offensive is very modest. Between 2002 and 2010, the state-owned share of total exports dropped from 37.9 percent to 14.9 percent, while the private firms rose dramatically from a meager 4.3 percent to 27.3 percent (Koopman, Wang, and Wei 2009; 21 Seiki Chugoku Soken 2011).

Foreign-affiliated companies are engaged mostly in processing exports (72.0 percent of their exports and 46.9 percent of China's total exports as of 2010 a [21 Seiki Chugoku Soken 2011]; both shares are declining), which means that the product is designed overseas and most of the inputs—materials, parts, components, and so on—are imported, while the value added by processing or assembly inside China is relatively small. Until recently, Chinese establishments of foreign firms have been largely focused on simple, labor-intensive operations at the final stages of the technological chains while more technologically sophisticated stages of the chain remained outside the country. Also, foreign firms often outsource particular stages of the production process to Chinese domestic manufacturers.

Domestic firms, especially in the private sector, are engaged mostly in ordinary exports, with most of the value of exported products created inside the country. In 2010, processing exports accounted for 9.8 percent of the total for private firms and 27.2 percent for SOE (21 Seiki Chugoku Soken 2011).

A New Role: China as a Leading Producer and Exporter of Parts and Components

The share of foreign value added in the ordinary exports is estimated to be 5–11 percent, and in the processing exports 74–82 percent. Exported computers, telecom equipment, and electronic devices have a foreign content of about 80 percent (Koopman, Wang, and Wei 2009). It would still be safe to say that, as a rule, the more technologically sophisticated the product is, the smaller its Chinese value-added portion tends to be.

However, this is an old story. Although its pages are not yet closed, a new story has begun. China steadily increases the value added created within its territory, developing upstream industries and hosting a growing number of stages of the production process. Foreign-owned producers of parts, materials, and other inputs are contributing a lot to this change, significantly expanding the range of their activities in the country. In a very important development, the country has already become a leading producer and exporter not only of final products, but also of parts and components, and is rapidly strengthening its position in this key segment (though, of course, their imports are much larger than exports).

For instance, between 2000 and 2009, China's production of integrated circuits (IC) soared from 5,880 million to 41,440 million units (21 Seiki Chugoku Soken 2010; Institute of Chinese Affairs 2011). In 2000, its exports of IC and electronic components was no more than $5,352 million compared to $62,824 million for the United States, $42,454 million for Japan, $24,688 million for South Korea, and $21,767 million for Taiwan. In 2009, the picture was entirely different. China increased its exports almost eight fold and ran second right after Taiwan ($40,328 million and $43,629 million respectively), overtaking the United States ($37,726 million), Japan ($36,563 million), and South Korea ($26,995 million) (WTO 2010).

Group Two Industries: China Is the Top Producer, but Not the Top Exporter

The second group consists of an array of key materials-producing industries, transportation machinery, nonelectrical (general) machinery, and a number of other sectors. Representative examples include nonferrous metals like copper and aluminum, cement, synthetic rubber, machine tools, auto vehicles and parts, precision instruments, pharmaceuticals, and so on. Currently the steel industry has also joined this group.

In these industries, China has rapidly risen to the position of the major producer, but has not become a leading exporter. They are targeting mostly the domestic market, and, as demand inside the country is expanding fast, retain a lot of room for further expansion in a similar fashion.

As a rule, in these sectors China is a big net importer. Although in the global markets Chinese manufacturers may exert a growing competitive pressure on their Western and other foreign counterparts, the latter get a big chance to capture a rapidly growing Chinese market.

Machine Tools and Motor Vehicles

For the Chinese economy, 2009 was a year of machine tools and motor vehicles: China became the world's top maker of both. We will pick them up as representative examples.

In both cases, in spite of leadership in production, China's position as an exporter remains modest.

Global exports of machine tools are dominated by German and Japanese firms. Also, China's imports are more than thrice as large as exports because domestic demand significantly exceeds domestic production (Table 4.6).

As for motor vehicles (Table 4.7), in 2000 China produced only about 2 million units, including 605,000 passenger cars, and exported nothing. Its production lagged far behind that of Japan, the United States, and Germany. In 2009, it already manufactured 13,791 thousand vehicles (including 10,384,000 passenger cars), 4.7 times more than in 2000 and about twice as much as the second-largest producer Japan. In 2010, the volume of production hit 18 million, or 23.4 of the world total (Cheng 2011).

Table 4.6   Production, Exports/Imports, and Domestic Use of Machine Tools (2009)

	Production	Exports	Imports	Domestic Use
China	15,000	1,400	5,800	19,400
Germany	10,249	7,203	2,225	5,451
Japan	7,095	4,219	443	3,319
United States	5,239	' 3,316	818	2,741
Italy	2,324	1,215	2,260	3,370
Switzerland	2,118	1,824	571	866
Spain	1,060	800	299	560
Taiwan	2,419	1,936	363	847
South Korea	2,665	1,212	1,133	2,586

$ million.
SOURCE: Sekai Kokusei Dzue 2009/2010.

Table 4.7   Production and Exports of Motor Vehicles

	2000		2009–2008	
	Production	Exports	Production	Exports
China	2,069 (605)	0	13,791 (10,384)	681
Japan	10,141 (8,359)	4,455	7,935 (6,862)	5,915
United States	12,800 (5,542)	1,477	5,709 (2,246)	1,966
Germany	5,527 (5,132)	3,723	5,210 (4,965)	4,501
Spain	3,033 (2,366)	1,317	2,170 (1,813)	2,181
France	3,348 (2,880)	3,619	5,709 (2,246)	4,322
South Korea	3,115 (2,602)	1,676	3,513 (3,158)	2,684
UK	1,814 (1,641)	1,159	1,090 (999)	1,254
India	801 (518)	44	2,633 (2,166)	526

In thousand units; in parentheses: production of passenger cars.
SOURCE: Sekai Kokusei Dzue 2010/2011.

However, China's motor vehicle exports, which started from 2003, remain meager: only 681,000 units in 2008 and 540,000 units in 2010 (Institute of Chinese Affairs 2011). The major exporters are Japan, the United States, Germany, France, and South Korea. With a few exceptions (most of all Honda), foreign subsidiaries operating in China are not that active globally, focusing on the production for the domestic market.

China's exports of all automotive products in 2009 (about $20 billion) were only less than half those of the United States ($45 billion), about a quarter of the EU-27's (extra-EU exports only: $78 billion), and less than one-fifth of Japan's ($103 billion) (WTO 2010).

Geely's acquisition of Volvo in 2009 shows that Chinese automakers are taking initial steps to establish a global position, but they still have a long way to go.

Steel Industry

In the second half of the 2000s, the steel industry joined group one, as China became the world leader in both production and exports.

In 2000, it produced 128.5 million metric tonnes of crude steel, or 15.1 percent of the world total, closely followed by Japan (106.4 million tonnes) and less closely by Russia (59.1 million tonnes) and others. In 2010, its production rose to 626.7 million tonnes, or 44.4 percent of the world total (World Steel Association 2010; International Steel Statistics Bureau 2011). Japan was at number two again with, respectively, 109.6 million tonnes and 7.8 percent, but the gap widened dramatically.

In the second half of the 2000s, China also rose to the position of the top exporter. In terms of value, in 2008 its steel exports hit $71.0 billion, or 27.1 percent of the world total against, respectively, $44.1 billion and 7.5 percent for Japan (WTO 2010).

However, in 2009 China's exports abruptly declined to just $24 billion. It descended to the position of the number four exporter and became a net steel importer like at the beginning of the decade.

It also ceded the position of the leading exporter of semifinished and finished steel products with exports falling by more than half from a year earlier (from $56,304 million to $23,639 million). In spite of the global demand squeeze, a decline in the exports from other countries was much smaller. Japan's exports decreased from $36,923 million to $33,306 million, and Russia's from $28,429 million to $27,587 million (WTO 2010).

In 2010, steel exports rebounded, boosted by the global economic recovery. However, China did not return to the top position, climbing up only to number two. It exported 38.8 million tonnes of crude steel compared to Japan's 42.4 million tonnes (International Steel Statistics Bureau 2011). Most of its production increment is absorbed by the domestic market. The steel industry currently remains in the group two.

Group Three Industries: China Is Neither the Top Producer Nor a Major Exporter

This group consists of a rather small number of industries, mostly materials-producing, where we don't find China among major exporters and where also, at least for the time being, it remains considerably or slightly behind the top producer—mostly the United States—in terms of production volumes. The major examples are basic petrochemicals and plastics.

For instance, as of 2008, China produced 10,240 thousand tonnes of ethylene (just 9.2 percent of the world total) against 23,554 thousand tonnes for the United States. The production of propylene amounted to, respectively, 9,520 thousand tonnes (13.5 percent) and 14,995 thousand tonnes, benzene 4,966 thousand tonnes (12.5 percent) and 6,561 thousand tonnes, and so on.

China's total production volume of the four major plastics (polyethylene, polypropylene, polystyrene, and polyvinyl chloride) combined was 26,920 thousand tonnes (16.8 percent of the world total) as opposed to America's 29,935 thousand tonnes.

Also, compared to the United States, China produced much less pulp: respectively 51,479 thousand tonnes and 21,477 thousand tonnes in 2008, and a little less paper: 79,952 thousand tonnes and 79,800 thousand tonnes (Yano Tsuneta Kinenkai 2011).

Key Features of China's Manufacturing Lead

Overall, today's China is leading in both production and exports of a wide and widening range of final goods, especially electronic/electrical products and light industry consumer items. It has also joined the ranks of major producers and exporters of electronic components.

On the other hand, its position as an exporter of materials is considerably weaker, even though it often leads in terms of production volumes. In a number of major materials-producing sectors, especially in the chemical industry, it lags rather far behind the top producer: the United States.

Also, for the time being, China has not established a significant presence in the global markets of machinery products other than electrical/electronic. Its production is growing fast, but producers are targeting primarily the domestic market. Western countries (as well as, often, newly developed economies like South Korea and Taiwan) have a much stronger position as exporters of motor vehicles and other automotive products, and major nonelectrical machinery goods like machine tools.

They also lead in the exports of scientific and controlling instruments, and pharmaceuticals.

Anatomy of China's Merchandise Trade Surplus

China exports much more than it imports.

However, notably, the range of its major trade surplus creators— among both industries and companies—is limited: It is, first of all, the industries of the group and domestic private firms, rapidly strengthening their global position and often squeezing out Western-based manufacturers.

China's surplus is also geographically biased: It is generated first and foremost by its trade with the West, having become an irritant in its relations with both the United States and European nations. However, in its trade with almost all major countries and territories of East Asia, as well as many other emerging and developing countries, China runs permanent deficits. This important fact often remains forgotten. In 2009, China had a $157.7 billion surplus in its merchandise trade with North America and a $112.3 billion surplus with Europe, but a $65.0 billion trade deficit with Asia and a $17.3 billion deficit with South and Central America (WTO 2010).

Net Exporter and Net Importer Sectors

China's trade surplus ($195.1 billion in 2009) is generated mostly by the group one industries: light industry goods including textiles, clothing, personal and household items, and miscellaneous manufactures (a combined surplus of $299.5 billion); office and telecom equipment (a surplus of $132.4 billion); and electrical machinery ($31.3 billion).

Industries belonging to group two and group three are usually big net importers. Representative examples include chemicals, machine tools, semiconductor-producing equipment, scientific and controlling instruments, and so on. Trade in automotive products is also in deficit, though it is small.

Also, dramatic expansion of China's production and exports of final goods is often accompanied by an almost equally dramatic increase of imports of key inputs indispensable for their manufacturing. For instance, China's net imports of integrated circuits (IC) and electronic parts hit $104.6 billion in 2008 and $95.6 billion in 2009 (WTO 2010).

However, overall, in its trade in intermediate products China shifted from a $3.4 billion deficit in 2001 to an impressive $106.3 billion surplus in 2008. In 2009 it registered a $3.5 billion deficit. Its parts and components trade surplus rose from $3.5 billion in 2001 to $21.7 billion in 2009 (RIETI 2010).

Domestic Private Companies Have Become the Major Surplus Creators

Chinese state-owned enterprises (SOEs) have become big net importers. In 2010, their imports were $153.2 billion larger than exports. In contrast, in an important new development, out of all types of companies, domestic private enterprises generated the largest trade surplus: $233.5 billion versus $88.3 billion for foreign-affiliated companies, though their volume of exports comprised only 56.6 percent of that of the latter (21 Seiki Chugoku Soken 2011).

The major reason is that, as mentioned, foreign-affiliated firms are still largely focused on processing exports.

The larger the volume of such exports, the more imports of foreign-made inputs are needed to sustain their growth. Consequently, nations and companies exporting those inputs enjoy a big opportunity. The key point is which regions, countries, and companies succeed in tapping China's dynamic market.

Note

1. All domestic Chinese companies other than state-owned and collectives were counted as private.

Chapter 5

Chinese Domestic Manufacturers versus Western Manufacturers

C hinese domestic companies have been strengthening their global position in several stages. To trace the logic of this change, we will divide all manufacturing products into four segments depending on the three criteria.

The Four Segments Analytical Framework

The first criterion is the level of technologies used and the technological intensity of production. For the sake of simplicity, products will be divided into low-tech and high-tech. In literature and statistical sources, the notions of high-tech and low-tech are quite flexible and vary depending on the author and the source. We assume that a high-tech product is one whose manufacturing requires advanced, complicated technologies and special technological skills for the majority of people involved in its production, which can be acquired only through special education and/or continuous professional training. On the contrary, production of low-tech items requires simpler technologies that can be mastered within a shorter period of time and without a solid special knowledge base.

Of course, these definitions are far from perfect—perfect definitions for *high-tech* and *low-tech*, as well as for *high-end* and *low-end* products hardly exist at all. As a rule some industries, such as electronics, precision machinery, or pharmaceuticals, are defined as high-tech; others, like textiles or chemicals, are not, but this division does not allow us to grasp differences among products and technological processes within every particular industry—for instance, to draw a distinction between a Braun tube TV and a plasma TV, though technologies required to manufacture the former may already not be that high; or between traditional chemical products and fine chemicals, though the latter's production technologies may be high indeed.

The second criterion is the product's grade. Products are divided into low-end and high-end (recently in the literature we also come across the notion of mid-range products, but here, to simplify the conceptual framework, we will include them in the low-end segment). *Low-end* means that the product is supposed to satisfy consumer's basic needs and does not pretend to bring a touch of sophistication and luxury. Foodstuffs are made to satisfy hunger, clothes to cover the human body, cars to let their users move from point A to point B, and phone apparatus to give and receive calls. Buyers expect them to properly perform those basic functions and don't attach too many additional demands. A high-end item, on the contrary, is purchased in order to enjoy sophistication and a touch of luxury. Such things as delicious taste, fashion, modern and beautiful design, quality of materials, comfort, or, if it is about capital goods like machine tools, numerical control function and high precision processing capability obtain primary importance.

Finally, the third criterion is the role of the name or the brand of a particular producer. There are mass products and differentiated products. When you buy the former, you don't care that much about who exactly has made them. They simply have to be acceptable in terms of quality and price. When you purchase the latter, you have in mind a particular producer or a brand that is associated with high quality, reliability, special design, unique product characteristics, and, generally, with the producer's image created through advertising and other marketing channels.

Using these criteria, we define four product segments:

1. Low-tech–low-end–mass products
2. High-tech–low-end–mass products
3. Low-end–differentiated products (both low-tech and high-tech)
4. High-end products (both low-tech and high-tech)

We assume that all high-end products are differentiated. Also, to reduce the number of segments for the sake of simplicity, in the third and the fourth segments we include both low-tech and high-tech products. It will not impede tracing the trends.

Chinese Manufacturers' Global Offensive: Four Stages

At this point, Chinese domestic producers have established themselves as leaders in the first segment of the global market. As a next step, they are rapidly expanding their presence in the second segment and are becoming recognizable in the third. Finally, they are approaching the fourth, high-end segment, too, with a few of them having grown into its important players. Yet, overall, their present position in the third and the fourth segments is still relatively weak.

Stage One: Low-Tech–Low-End Mass Products

The first stage started with the launch of the openness and reform policies in the late 1970s to early 1980s. Chinese makers established themselves as dominant players in the production and exports of a wide variety of *low-tech–low-end mass* products, defeating producers of similar items in the West. Myriads of Chinese-made cheap T-shirts, sneakers, lighters, toys, kitchenware, and so on and so forth conquered markets all around the world.

In this segment, where price makes all the difference, Western producers are doomed to lose. Nowadays China's dominance here is continuing, in spite of the fact that its rising labor and other costs have become a hot topic worldwide.

There is a lot of talk about the erosion of its cost advantage resulting in the shift of low-cost mass production to the countries of the next row like Vietnam, Bangladesh, Sri Lanka, Cambodia, or Laos. The only option for China, according to this school of thought, is to upgrade its industries and produce more high-value-added goods. This is wrong. China is unique. It will not be shifting from lower-value-added to higher-value-added products. It will handle *both*. In other words, China is and, for decades to come, will be moving up and up the value chain on the one hand while retaining its dominance in the low-tech–low-end segment on the other. In this regard, it is different from any other nation. Its growth pattern goes beyond the famous flying geese framework in its conventional sense.

China's ability to preserve dominance in the low-tech–low-end mass products segment can be easily explained. First, its labor and other costs are still quite low. They remain incomparable with those in the West and thus do not lose attractiveness for both Western businesses and consumers. Second, no next-row country can compare with China in terms of size. Consequently, none of them is capable of replacing it as the major production platform for low-end simple products, even though their costs are lower.

True, more and more often both Western and Asian business-people are complaining about the increase of China's labor and other costs, and the mass media is willingly picking it up as a popular topic. However, read or listen to what they say attentively, word by word, and you will clearly see what it is all about. They are upset that today Chinese costs are higher than in past years and higher than they initially expected them to be. Nevertheless, they continue to expand their direct investment to China on a much larger scale than to any next-row country. Actions, not talks, are serving as proof of China's real cost competitiveness.

According to a study by the Boston Consulting Group, China's average wage rate in manufacturing, adjusted for productivity, rose from 36 percent of that in the United States in 2000 to 48 percent in

2010 (Powell 2011), which means that its cost advantages remain very significant.

Also, you should bear in mind that national average cost indicators may be misleading due to enormous differences among the regions. Though wage growth rates are high all across China (around 10 percent a year), labor (as well as other) costs are starting to bite, mainly in the economically advanced eastern coastal provinces. (Yet, even there, with the exception of Shanghai and Beijing, they still usually comprise no more than a fraction of those in the West.) On the contrary, in the hinterland's central, northeastern, and western provinces, with a few exceptions, they remain competitive enough even by the standards of the developing world.

As of 2009, employees' average monthly wage for all regions of China stood at $393. In Shanghai it was $712, in Beijing $704. In the western and central provinces it was mostly within a $320–$360 range; for instance, $320 in Hubei (central) and Yunnan (west), $350 in Anhui (central), and $360 in Shaanxi (west) (author's calculations based on National Bureau of Statistics 2010a). Employees' average monthly wage in the United States in 2008 was about $3,800 (U.S. Census Bureau 2011a).

The average hourly wage in China's manufacturing industry is still about $3.10—versus $22.30 in the United States, though in the eastern provinces it is up to 50 percent higher (Powell 2011).

China's growth does not fit the conventional flying geese pattern because it is unveiling its domestic version. While eastern coastal provinces, pressed by rising costs, are climbing up the value chain, inland provinces still have room to grow fast, producing simple products and exploiting low-cost advantages. (It does not mean, however, that they cannot simultaneously upgrade their industries—they can and they do.) Also, big cities in the east are becoming service, logistics, education, and R&D platforms, supporting industrial growth in the hinterland.

Notably, inland provinces are becoming China's main growth engines. At least since 2008, the center and the west have been growing faster than the eastern coastal areas. For example, while in 2009 the national economy as a whole grew 9.2 percent, growth rates in the central provinces of Anhui (with populations of 61 million), Hubei

(57 million), and Henan (94 million) hit 12.9 percent, 13.2 percent and 10.6 percent respectively, and the fastest runner was the western autonomous region of Inner Mongolia with a growth rate of 19 percent. The shift of growth centers from coastal provinces to the hinterland is gaining additional strength from state-sponsored development projects in the central and especially western regions. They were the major beneficiaries of the famous 4 trillion yuan stimulus package unveiled in 2008. Also, they are becoming increasingly important investment targets for both domestic and foreign companies.

These provinces are in a good position to expand production of low-tech–low-end mass items both for the domestic and the external market. Currently their industries are oriented mostly toward the domestic market, but emerging excellent export opportunities are unlikely to be missed.

As far as the countries' size and the scale of their economies are concerned, most next-row states are comparable to no more than a single Chinese province.

No doubt, as time goes by, they will significantly enhance their international role as producers and exporters and attract a growing number of multinational companies pursuing the China plus one (or plus two, or plus three) strategy to expand and diversify the geography of their production activities. Sometimes multinationals even choose to relocate production from China to other countries, and it may have important repercussions for a particular industry. For instance, in 2005, after the United States imposed tariffs on Chinese-made wooden bedroom furniture, many of its Taiwanese and other makers made up their minds to move from China to Vietnam, not least because there they have to pay a furniture worker $80 a month rather than $170 in China (in the United States it is $12 per hour). In the latter half of the decade, Vietnam overtook China as this item's leading exporter to the United States (Higgins 2011).

With the rising role of the next-row countries and the moves of particular companies to relocate there, production of particular goods looks sensational and often turns outs to be in the focus of the public attention. However, they do not mean that China as a whole is challenged as the world's number one manufacturing platform for low-cost simple products. Size differentials with potential challengers are too big.

Perhaps, the only next-row country with a potential to challenge China in terms of the manufacturing production scale could be India, but it still has a very long way to go. Its export-oriented low-cost manufacturing remains relatively weak, and overall manufacturing output, as mentioned, currently accounts for no more than one-tenth that of China.

So, as there is no challenger around, in the low-tech–low-end mass products segment China retains its edge. However, it does not mean that it keeps production costs and prices as low as in the past. It is exactly the reverse. Being a de facto monopolist, China has room, up to a certain point, to raise prices for these products to cover its growing production costs.

At the start of the second decade of the twenty-first century, consumers around the world continue to actively buy "made-in-China" simple mass products, even though they have to pay somewhat more than before. In this segment, it is the major trend. All the rest is secondary.

Stage Two: High-Tech–Low-End Mass Products

In the second stage, which started in the 1990s and has been continuing into the 2000s and beyond, Chinese companies are moving fast to capture global markets of technologically advanced low-end mass products, leveraging their increasing technological capabilities and cost advantages at one and the same time. Representative examples include TVs, AV products, mobile phones, personal computers, or, in the latest development, solar batteries.

Entering this sector, Chinese makers exert competitive pressure on the Western companies positioned in higher-end market niches, usually by offering simpler versions of similar products at a lower price.

Three recent breakthroughs reflecting this new trend are especially important.

First, China has emerged as the world's number one producer of solar panels. Today, 5 out of their 10 top world makers are Chinese domestic firms. Within the two years to 2010, prices for Chinese-made solar panels dropped by about half. It enables China to play a leading role in the global energy revolution as such drastic price cuts drive solar energy costs down toward the grid parity level, where the prices of renewable and conventional energy become equal.

Between 2005 and 2010, Chinese makers conquered 43 percent of the global market of photovoltaic panels. In a $10 million project, the country's second-largest maker, Yingli Green Energy, supplied 7,600 solar panels to New Jersey's Rutgers University for the biggest solar power experiment at a U.S. college (Biggs 2010).

Second, dissemination of electric vehicles provided strong momentum for growth of China's lithium-ion battery industry. In their recent conversations with the author, managers of Japanese companies working in the same field acknowledged, one after another, that in both quantitative and qualitative terms, China's progress appears to be much faster than they initially expected. In 2007, according to Xinhua, its production of lithium-ion batteries (1.4 billion packs) reached more than one-third of the world total. Top makers like Shenzhen-based BYD and BAK Battery are significantly improving the batteries' safety and reliability. Tianjin Lishen Battery, the world's sixth-largest producer, has become a partner supplier for the leading electronic makers such as Samsung and Motorola. In parallel, a number of its smaller manufacturers are expanding the supply of low-capacity batteries for cell phones and MP3 players (*Beijing Review* 2009).

An additional impetus for China's leadership in this area comes from the fact that its lithium reserves are the third-largest in the world after Chile and Argentina.

Third, China is rapidly increasing its presence in the global market for power equipment, especially in the emerging world. Its leading producers, Shanghai Electric and Harbin Power Equipment, are competing directly with General Electric and other Western giants. One of the breakthrough developments was the signing by Shanghai Electric of a $10 billion contract with India's Reliance Power to supply coal-fired generators—probably the world's largest contract ever for generators.

Stage Three: Low-End–Differentiated Products

At the third stage, the Chinese are starting to pursue differentiation of their products: both low-tech and high-tech. One of their most popular tools to achieve this goal is buying the brands of internationally famous Western companies, along with acquiring their product departments, initiating tie-up arrangements, or, more and more often, acquiring them altogether. The trend gained strength in the 2000s.

Lenovo became famous for its acquisition of the PC department of IBM in 2004. It made its own name recognizable all around the world and effectively contributed to the establishment of the Lenovo brand associated with an attractive cost-quality mix, dynamism, entrepreneurial spirit, newcomer's aggressiveness (in the positive meaning of the word), quick learning, desire to innovate, openness, and readiness to integrate different business cultures.

Having invested more than $500 million, the country's second-largest TV maker TCL established a joint venture with the French electronic giant Thomson and became its majority partner. Thomson also owns the world-famous American brand RCA. The tie-up opened the way for producing under both Thomson and RCA brands and was also used to promote products under the brand of TCL itself, though mostly in the Third World countries. Then, through its subsidiary, TCL also acquired the cellular phone business of Alcatel.

Pearl River Piano, controlling 60 percent of China's piano market, acquired a small British maker exporting pianos under the German brand Ritmuller (Williamson 2004).

However, buying the brand is not at all an easy and not necessarily a successful game. Its costs are very high—especially as Chinese firms usually target famous but ailing companies or poorly performing product divisions their Western counterparts are eager to sell. Thus, as a rule, Chinese acquirers have to bear a heavy financial burden without any guarantee that the company or the division they have purchased will be put back on track.

TCL's venture has been in the red from the very start.

Lenovo's profit margins are extremely low, and it is pressed back by Dell, HP, and Acer. In 2006, due to its poor performance, the Hong Kong Exchange removed it from the list of companies included in the key Hang Seng Index.

In another development, step-by-step, slowly but surely, a cohort of domestic companies is gradually establishing international brands of their own, without embarking on costly acquisitions.

For instance, sports apparel maker Li Ning is challenging Nike and Adidas in terms of design and product selection. In January 2010, it opened its first retail store in Portland, Oregon. Furthermore, it started design operations near Nike's headquarters in Beaverton, Oregon, hiring American personnel (Rein 2010).

Tsingtao Brewery has become a popular name in many countries of the world as one of the symbols of the Chinese taste.

Other examples of increasingly recognizable Chinese brands include air-conditioner producer Midea, telecom equipment maker ZTE, car makers Chery and Geely, clean technology company LDK Solar, and so on.

In the West it is often argued that, with a few exceptions, Chinese companies are lacking brand-building capabilities. Sometimes it is even considered proof that China is not an economic superpower.

This argument is not convincing. True, China's progress in this area is much slower than in others. However, besides the evidence of progress already achieved, we have to take into account the fact that most Chinese companies that are seriously working on differentiating their products are establishing brands in their own way, going through several stages. They start not from America, Europe, or Japan, but from China itself: the most rapidly expanding and the most familiar market in the world. Then they move or will move on to other developing countries, taking advantage of the markets' dynamism and comparatively weak competition from other brand-builders. In the Third World they can also capitalize on their still relatively low production and sales costs. And only after that, having acquired brand-building skills and experience, some of them will go to America, Europe, Japan, and other developed states.

The interviews conducted by the China Market Research Group with several hundred senior executives of Chinese consumer goods–making companies, showed that over 50 percent of the respondents expected to enter the United States in five years, but only after they target their home market and regions like Africa and the Middle East (Rein 2010). If they realize their plans, in the second half of this decade Chinese and Western brands will start genuinely competing in the U.S. territory.

Stage Four Is Coming: Chinese Makers Are on the Threshold of the High-End Segment

The fourth stage is coming. Some Chinese companies are beginning to target the high-end products segment.

The probability is high that by the end of this decade people around the world will come to know well a group of at least a dozen Chinese producers of nonelectrical and electrical machinery, electronic goods, apparel products, and so on, with internationally recognized brands, respected for high quality and originality of their sophisticated products. And even in the high-end sector the Chinese may also exploit their cost advantage.

The emergence and expansion of such a cohort will be fostered by several driving forces.

To begin with, China money is at work. Many Chinese firms have earned a great deal selling low-end goods, and are now heavily investing in products' upgrading and technological innovation. Quite often they get significant financial support from the government.

Second, with a lot of cash at hand, they are beginning to attract the best talent from around the world: designers, researchers, engineers, and managers. The trend will gain strength.

At the same time, the pool of high-skilled Chinese cadres, ready for high-end jobs, is widening too—both due to improvements in the educational system and the increase in the number of Chinese choosing to return home after studying and/or working in the West.

Third, to speed up production upgrading, Chinese firms are using their new financial strength to purchase parts, components, machinery, and equipment manufactured by the world's best producers.

The machine tools industry provides a valuable example of China's drive toward the high end.

As mentioned, in 2009 China became the largest producer of machine tools in the world. Until recently, however, it produced rather simple and cheap machines, while the high-end segment was dominated by German, Japanese, Italian, Swiss, and other makers from industrially developed countries. Having a sharp technological edge, the latter commanded high prices for their products.

However, since mid-2000s things have begun to change. In 2004, one of the leading Chinese makers, Shenyang Machine Tool Group

(SMTCL), acquired Germany's Schiess AG, which announced bank-ruptcy earlier the same year. Within a short time, European designers and engineers noticeably improved SMTCL's products. The company rapidly increased the number of Japanese-made parts and components installed. It started to establish the image of a globally oriented pro-ducer of advanced precision machine tools, working hard to overcome users' mistrust rooted in the concerns about made-in-China's poor quality. Currently it supplies flat-bed CNC machining centers and other products to customers in the United States, Canada, the United Kingdom, Italy, Spain, India, South Africa, and so on.

The most famous examples of Chinese companies knocking at the high-end segment door are the 2Hs—Huawei and Haier.

Huawei, the world's second-largest network and telecom equip-ment supplier in the world after Ericsson, serves 31 out of the 50 larg-est telecom operators around the globe (Griffin 2007). It was chosen by British Telecom as a preferred supplier for its 21 CN network strategy in 2005 and awarded the Vodaphone Award for Outstanding Performance in 2007. It launched a joint venture with the UK's Global Marine Systems to deliver undersea network equipment (Wang 2008) and signed an agreement with Germany's third-largest fixed-line oper-ator Versatel to build a fiber optic communication network based on Internet Protocol (*China Daily* 2006).

Its latest breakthrough was the development of a mid-level Android 2.2 smartphone (powered by a Qualcomm MSM7230800 MHz processor, with a 3.8″ capacitive TFT 480 × 800 screen; 5Mp camera; 720p recording playback). Initially it targeted the mid-range market, but, as of early 2011 began to be compared favorably with high-end phones, posing a challenge for their makers by a very com-petitive price of $250 to $300. Right after, the company announced the X6 model with a 1 Ghz processor and a 4.1″ screen (Atkinson 2011; Westaway 2011).

Haier has become a world-famous producer of a range of house-hold appliances, from air-conditioners to TVs. It commands the world's largest market share in white goods. In 2010, Euromonitor International ranked it first in three categories: refrigeration appli-ances, home laundry, and electrical wine cooler/chiller appliances (Jones 2010). Having developed an array of original products, it is successfully competing in the medium and high-end market segments in the United States, Europe, and many developing countries, emphasizing stylishness and modernity, functionality, reliability, and the use of the very latest technologies—all this in combination with affordable prices. The Haier advertisement catches your eye when you stroll through the famous Ginza-4 Crossing in Tokyo, in the very center of Japan's most lush area.

Western Manufacturers: A New Way of Thinking Is Required

A memory of a very recent past. Several years ago, amid heated debates about the undervalued yuan and China's currency manipulation, one of America's major TV channels interviewed an owner-manager of a socks-making company. He was bitterly complaining that he would not keep afloat if yuan did not appreciate and Chinese-made socks continued to sell for some 65 cents a pair. I understood his feelings. However, the more I listened to his talk, the more I felt that he was not on the right track: The yuan appreciation, perhaps, might somewhat ease his pain for a certain period of time, but, unfortunately, could not provide a solution.

According to various estimates, the yuan is currently undervalued by 40–60 percent. Even if a miracle happens and its exchange rate goes up 60 percent right away, cost differentials between China and the United States will remain significant, as the average wage of a Chinese worker in the manufacturing industries is currently less than one-seventh that of his U.S. colleague (and the socks-producing industry is hardly an exception). The mentality has to change. Time has come to realize that U.S.-based makers of socks for everyday use are no longer in a position to compete with their Chinese counterparts—be it at their domestic market or anywhere else. Furthermore, it is hardly relevant and desirable for America to force its consumers to pay more for their everyday-wear socks—not least because for many of them global competition exerts strong downward pressure on wages.

One more example from the recent past. In the mid-2000s, U.S. bedroom furniture makers formed the American Furniture

Manufacturers Committee for Legal Trade and began to press the government to give them protection from Chinese exports, insisting that they threatened "our way of life, our culture and the competitiveness of America in the world." Really confusing. So high and passionate wording was obviously in contradiction with the harsh reality, namely the racket to buy protection. Chinese makers paid cash to their American competitors who had the right to ask the U.S. Ministry of Commerce to review import duties. References to values and culture are hardly relevant. It rather resembles the world depicted in *The Godfather* by Mario Puzo.

But let us return to the four segments scheme. The point is that there is no more economic rationale for U.S. and other Western-based factories to produce goods belonging to the first and also, increasingly, the second segment. This is the golden rule of the globalized economy. In a sense, they don't have *the right* to produce them (it is not about a legal right, of course, but about the right stemming from economic common sense, and maybe even about the moral right if you assume that producers have to serve the society—don't they?), because Chinese and other Third World factories can provide the same customer value at a lower price (to repeat—even if the yuan becomes 1.5 times or even twice as heavy as it is now). Consequently, Western governments basically don't have the "right" to protect such producers by higher tariffs and other means, because it will harm the vast majority of their countries' households.

If you play by the rules of the globalized economy, the only genuine solution for a Western-based manufacturer can be a shift to the third or the fourth segment: in other words, product differentiation. Trying to compete with Chinese-made products on price is mostly meaningless. In today's world, whether a Western-based factory has the "right" and the rationale to continue operating, depends on its ability to produce differentiated products—preferably those that are in demand internationally because the domestic market may be too small.

If you want to continue making socks in the United States, try to make them character goods, think of a peculiar design attractive for particular groups of customers, bet on special features like high durability, sweat-absorbing ability, or whatever. It is advisable to shift from regular socks as a mass product to high-grade socks as a fashion item and to do your best to establish the brand. If you want to produce bedroom furniture, develop strong attractive American brands, popular not only in the United States but also around the world and capable of competing with internationally recognized Italian, French, Spanish, or Swedish makers. Otherwise you are doomed to lose, and the yuan appreciation won't be of help.

The emergence of China as a major competitor brings about a deep polarization in the global manufacturing industry, creating three groups of winners and one group of losers. The winners are Chinese domestic companies, Western multinationals using China as a production platform, and Western non-multinationals making differentiated, especially high-end products and increasing their exports to rapidly expanding markets in China and other developing countries. The losers are numerous unrecognizable non-multinational companies in the West making mass products: largely, but not only, small and medium-size firms. The key issue is how the latter can address the challenge and what policy can help them to succeed.

Let us have a deeper look at the options they have.

Option One: Stay at Home and Differentiate the Product

The first option is to pursue aggressive product differentiation: in other words, to shift from the first or the second to the third or, even better, to the fourth segment, establishing a position as a high-end goods maker. If you are a domestic market-oriented company, development of external markets is indispensable to expand the range of customers.

However, it is more easily said than done. Many Western businesses are simply unprepared for it both psychologically—lacking the will and persistence to work hard to achieve the goal—and organizationally: most of all due to the shortage of capable human resources, both at the managerial and the shop-floor level. Yes, the developed West has to make a very, very big step forward in human capacity building to train people capable of transforming its struggling companies and industries.

The shift from mass to differentiated, especially high-end products making is usually a difficult and risky thing. You have to find or newly create your group of customers and appeal to them so that they become fond of your brand name. You have to persuade people to pay more for every unit of your product than they did before. The number of buyers in your home country will inevitably become smaller, so you will have to expand or newly create your customer base overseas, including remote Third World countries whose markets are most dynamic. Most likely, you will have to make a tremendous effort and to bear a lot of expense to introduce more advanced technologies and more state-of-the-art equipment, to employ more high-skilled workers, to develop various product promotion channels, and so on—and you will have to do all this while you still remain in terra incognita, not knowing whether your potential customers will react in a positive way or not. Finally, the high-end product niches are usually already occupied by world-famous brand makers, which will make your mission even more challenging.

Presumably, product differentiation, especially a shift to the fourth, high-end products segment, can be handled only by a small portion of Western companies, and those who fail to access the limited market space will be squeezed out or, for the best, will have to struggle to make ends meet.

The process has already started.

A narrow circle of successful Western factories are differentiating their products and establishing a strong global position—largely (but not only) in the high-end products segment, while most domestic producers, especially small and medium, are either washed out or clutching to a straw. The overall number of manufacturers is falling.

Take Japan, famous for its strong manufacturing base. On the one hand, a cohort of small and medium-size domestic manufacturers is successfully capturing or even monopolizing important niches of the global market due to their outstanding technological capabilities, vigorous quality control, dynamic innovation, and persistent market development in various parts of the world. Nippon Ceramic is the world leader in the production of infrared sensors for security systems. Teibo manufactures about half of the world's fiber pen nibs, praised by NASA for their ability to write in space. Nakashima Propeller controls the lion's share of the global market for supersize screws for ships, and JAMCO for the lavatories for passenger planes. On the other hand, the overall number of manufacturing companies is decreasing, including companies belonging to the famous manufacturing clusters, like Ota Ward in Tokyo or Higashi-Osaka (Eastern Osaka) in the Osaka Prefecture. Traditionally, clusters of this kind generated strong synergy effects stemming from regular intercompany interactions and networking, and contributed a lot to the country's competitiveness in manufacturing. However, as much as 40 percent of companies in those cluster areas closed down in the 20 years prior to 2006 (Maruyama 2010).

Lots of manufacturers are frustrated. For instance, Japanese mold models (prototypes that produce objects) makers who were world leaders some 10 or even 5 years ago, are now facing strong competition from Chinese and Korean rivals, which appears to be very difficult if not impossible to overcome. In real life, more and more small entrepreneurs and their employees are left with no choice but to retreat and accept low-paid jobs in the service sector or even to shift (back?) to such traditional occupations as fishing to earn their living.

Option Two: Move to China

The second option for Western producers is transferring production to China and other emerging market countries to cut costs and raise price competitiveness. In other words, to go multinational. More and more firms, not only large, but also small and medium, are stepping along this road. The number of multinational small and medium-size manufacturers in America, Europe, and Japan is increasing at a remarkable speed—not least because of the Chinese challenge.

The emergence of strong micro-multinationals is an important global trend. According to the UN, in 1990 the total number of multinational companies was about 30,000. By the mid-2000s, it doubled while their average size fell (Copeland 2006). The majority of today's MNCs are not business giants, but small and medium companies—and, more and more frequently, manufacturing micro-multinationals from industrially developed states shift their production to China and other emerging countries, seeking to cut production costs.

However, for their home countries, without the expansion on a comparable scale of new manufacturing activities, such multinational-ization poses a threat of the hollowing-out of domestic industries and significant job losses (even though opening of a factory overseas creates some additional jobs at home, especially office jobs needed to coordinate, support, and monitor its activities).

The interests of multinationals and the countries of their origin become less and less identical. In the past it was taken for granted that everything that is good for General Motors is good for America. Nowadays it is not so: Not regarding GM, but at the most basic level—a country is one thing and a business organization is another. The performance of every country's manufacturing sector, its national economy as a whole and the well-being of its citizens increasingly depend on its ability to attract manufacturing and other companies from all around the world—China being one of the most vivid examples in this regard.

Western Governments Have to Initiate an Export Counteroffensive

So, both options described may work well for particular Western companies, but they pose big problems for Western economies as a whole, narrowing their domestic manufacturing base and worsening the employment environment. No easy solutions are in sight. However, these problems can and should be tackled more actively at the national policy level.

What can be done?

To begin with, the West has to accept that trying to keep its ailing industries afloat by pressing China to appreciate the yuan will not provide a genuine solution. (Though it does not mean that the West should not press China to appreciate yuan—it should, but for a different reason; we will come back to this point later on.) Protectionist measures like punitive import tariffs are an even worse an option. Doing effectively nothing to protect industries, they create risks of trade wars, harm consumers, and send the wrong signal to domestic producers: wrong because today it is basically more efficient to produce mass products in China than in the West.

Two closely interrelated strategies are vital to address the challenges posed by China's export offensive.

First, Western governments have to do more to encourage differentiation and upgrading of products by domestic factories (in other words, to help them shift from segments one and two to segments three and four), in order to expand the cohort of domestic manufacturers, especially SME, with high non-price competitiveness. The task of primary importance is to promote exports of such upgraded and differentiated products, especially to China and other emerging countries.

If an active export promotion policy is not in place, market constraints can critically weaken companies' motivation to differentiate and upgrade and, as a result, erode the technological base the West has already created, threatening its command over core manufacturing technologies.

Here is a quote from a conference address by Haruhisa Gai, the president of Tsubamex, a well-known Japanese manufacturer of mold models and the first company in the industry that introduced a three-dimensional CAD-CAM system to speed up product development and raise its quality. The topic under discussion was globalization and challenges from Chinese and other companies from the emerging world. Mr. Gai said:

> Costs aside, today there are only two countries in the world that can make any kind of a prototype: Japan and America. Even Germany cannot produce certain customized models. The level of Japan's manufacturing technologies is very high, but these days there is no work—and makers do not introduce new machines. If there are no new machines, no new technologies will be born. It is a very big problem. . . . One of our major headaches is that even if we get orders it is uncertain whether we will get the payment in due course—especially from overseas. It is very difficult to collect the money we have to be paid. It would be nice if this can be done by the state. . . . We count a lot on our links with overseas, but there are a lot of obstacles. (Chiiki Kasseika Jyanaru 2011)

The fragment quoted brilliantly articulates the problem and expresses concerns existing in Japan's business community.

To address the Chinese challenge, Western governments have to orchestrate a large-scale export counteroffensive on the Chinese market. In broader terms, they have to come out with a wide-range export promotion policy, centered on those domestic small and medium-size producers that are really capable of differentiating their products and climbing up the value chain. The promotion package can include far more active assistance in market research and sales promotion, in the establishment of overseas distribution channels, in the arrangement of trade fairs and other similar events, and so on. Publish and distribute beautiful goods catalogs in Chinese. Organize meetings and seminars with Chinese distribution industry people. Stage advertising campaigns. Don't be shy about allocating sufficient budget funds for these purposes. And, of course, do all you can to make China reduce its tariff and nontariff import barriers.

Much more can be done at the local administration level. Establish and expand direct province-to-province and city-to-city relations. (How many American and European cities have sister relations with Chinese cities? Not too many, really.) Organize various public events, and let the Chinese audiences know how good and attractive the products from your homeland are. They will be interested, without any doubt. Establish trade representative offices—and not only in Beijing and Shanghai, but also in other Chinese cities, effectively acting as export agents for your homeland's producers and their associations.

Finally, studying the feasibility of the U.S.-China and the EU-China free trade agreements would be a good idea. Can American and European leaders show enough vigor and courage to come out with such strategic initiatives? (Japan and South Korea are already working with China on a trilateral FTA, and the process seems to be gaining momentum.) It may not be as simple as endless debates about currency manipulators, but it is worth trying.

The range of options is wide. Without drastic steps of this kind, the West's deficits in its trade with China will continue to increase, and more and more Western manufacturers will have to bring down the curtain.

Chapter 6

A Big Battle for the Chinese Market

Abig battle for the Chinese market is starting.

In 2009, China became not only the world's top exporter, but also the second-largest importer. It is the number one market for an increasing amount of both capital and consumer goods. For instance, its share of the world market of optical fibers has hit 50 percent, and machine tools 30 percent (Shintaku 2010). In 2009, its portion of the world's imports of integrated circuits (IC) and electronic components reached 33 percent (WTO 2010). It is the largest market for cars and brand fashion goods and is about to become the number one for luxury goods. The list can be continued.

Yet, the competition for tapping this market is becoming increasingly fierce, and more often than not Western companies appear to be not on the winning side.

China-Bound Exports of Capital Goods: East Asia Is Leading

In the capital goods sector, the leading exporters to China are not American or European firms, but their East Asian, especially Japanese, South Korean, and Taiwanese competitors. Between 2000 and 2008, exports of final capital goods from East Asia (Japan, South Korea, Taiwan, and the ASEAN states) to China increased 6.2 times and reached $88,277 million against respectively 2.3 times and $16,990 million for the United States and 4.0 times and $39,014 million for the EU-15.

In the exports of parts and components the gaps are even more striking. Within the same period, East Asia increased its exports 5.9 times to $157,792 million, the United States 3.7 times to $16,881 million, and the 15 EU states 3.2 times to $32,049 million (RIETI 2010). Japan alone exported to China more parts and components than the whole EU-15 and more than twice as much as the United States. (East Asia's exports include those by local subsidiaries of American and European multinationals, but the lion's share is accounted for by the region's firms themselves.)

Not surprisingly, while enjoying enormous surpluses in its trade with America and Europe, China runs deficits in trade with almost all major countries and territories of East Asia, supporting their growth as the region's major market creator.

China-Bound Exports of Consumer Goods: Opportunities Are There, but You Have to Work Hard Not to Miss Them

China is rapidly establishing itself as the world's largest market for an increasing number of consumer products, from cars to cosmetics. According to RIETI, in 2007 its imports of consumer goods amounted to $33 billion—still small compared to $550 billion for the United States, $210 billion for Germany, or $120 billion for Japan. However, the pace of their expansion is remarkable: They were 3.6 times greater than in 2000. China is importing more and more food products, automobiles, computers, interior goods, kitchenware, sporting goods, and many other items.

New export opportunities for Western firms are opened by rising incomes of Chinese households and the expansion of the middle class, eager to improve its living standards and keen to imitate Western-style consumption patterns. These people are willing to buy Western-made goods to taste the real thing.

China is already the number one importer of many Western world-famous brand products. A key to invigorating Western manufacturing industry is, however, the ability of a wider range of consumer goods makers—not just a narrow circle of world-famous brands—to establish a position in the Chinese market. Especially, it refers to small and medium companies. They are not as famous as Armani, Versace, or Gucci, but for them the country name as such (made in Italy, or in France, or in Spain) may, at least to some extent, work as a brand substitute, while their selling prices can be lower than those for famous brand items.

China Trap

However, beware of a China trap.

On an average, prices in China are still much lower than in the West. Usually two markets exist for one and the same kind of product, effectively separated from one another. The major market, with Chinese prices, is dominated by domestic companies. The other market, on a smaller scale, is for Western products (including products made by Chinese subsidiaries of Western firms) with Western selling prices.

The vast majority of the Chinese families, belonging to the middle class by Chinese standards, do not have middle-class incomes by Western standards. Thus, their purchasing power is insufficient to buy Western goods for Western prices on a regular basis.

The bottom line for an annual income of a Chinese family belonging to the middle class varies depending on the source. It is often set at $3,000. In its recent survey (the results announced in 2006), McKinsey defined the Chinese middle class as households making 25,000–100,000 yuan (real yuan 2000, 1 yuan = $0.12), or $3,000–$12,000 a year. Their share of the total amount of urban households, which was 22 percent in 2005, is expected to reach 70.9 percent in 2015 and 79.2 percent in 2025.

It also introduced the notion of mass affluent households, group with annual income above 100,000 yuan and up to 200,000 yuan, or $12,000 and $24,000 respectively (Farrell 2006). Their portion of the total number of urban households is expected to rise from 0.5 percent in 2005 to 5.6 percent in 2015 and to 7.7 percent in 2025. Only incomes that are very close to the upper limit for the mass affluent group—$24,000 a year ($2,000 a month)—are somewhat comparable to the average income from work of an employed person in a developed country. Consequently, for Western exporters even this group is largely out of reach as a regular buyer of their products.

It would be different if the yuan exchange rate were higher. A weak yuan is a tool that is used by the Chinese state not only to encourage exports, but also—perhaps even more important—to shut out imports. This is the main reason why the West should continue pressing Beijing to speed up the appreciation process.

Chinese families belonging to the middle class and even to the mass affluent group have raised their living standards to the present level mostly by purchasing goods at Chinese prices produced by domestic makers. Domestic, not foreign, manufacturers are the major beneficiaries of China's middle-class expansion.

Only wealthy Chinese families (in the McKinsey model, the households with an annual income over 200,000 yuan, or $24,000), which by Western standards belong mostly to the middle class, enjoy the purchasing power, sufficient to buy West-made goods as a habit.

This group is small—1.6 million households as of the end of 2008, but rapidly expanding: Its growth rate is about 16 percent a year. By 2015 it is expected to reach 4 million households (McKinsey 2009a).

Obviously, its expansion is widening opportunities for Western producers/exporters, but scale constraints are significant.

At-Home Chinese Companies Are Active in the High-End Niche

Also, in this market for the wealthy, including the high-end products segment, competition with domestic companies is going to be really tough. The assumption that Chinese firms are mostly commanding the low-end product segment while Western manufacturers comfortably occupy the high-end one, may still stand for the global market, but already does not apply to the market of China itself.

Chinese firms are actively upgrading their products, improving their quality, and establishing brands. At this point, their activities of this kind are targeting mostly domestic customers. In the domestic market they have important advantages over Western competitors: proximity to the marketplace, absence of cultural and language barriers, and better knowledge of local customers' preferences—not to say that, while upgrading their products and building brands, they still enjoy a substantial cost advantage. Unlike overseas, inside the country their names are known not less if not more than those of their Western counterparts. All this puts them in a good position to expand.

Let us take the furniture market as a representative example.

On the one hand, Western firms are noticeably increasing their presence. Top brands like G. Versace, ColomboMobili, Fendi, or Rubelli have made their entries. The largest U.S. furniture maker Haworth has started production in Shanghai, and the three largest sofa makers of Italy have also set up their Chinese factories (DHMQ 2010). The U.S. brand Fine Furniture Design opened a flagship store in Beijing, followed by the Italian brand Savio Firmino.

On the other hand, however, domestic makers are moving remarkably fast to establish themselves as leading and immediately recognizable players in the high-end market niche. Shanghai-based Yun Dian Furniture offers furniture of the traditional Chinese style, often adding a little bit of Western flavor. In addition, it has found one more way to differentiate: All its pieces are made in mahogany. Foshan Jihao Furniture located at Lojiang town 40 kilometers from Guangzhou, has established a reputation as a high-end sofa manufacturer possessing such brand names as Menoir, Kouma, Kamina, and Sofia. Well known in China, it has also independently developed brands in South Korea, Spain, Australia, and Poland (Menoir Casa 2011). Dongguan-based maker Fu Yi Furniture opened a 1,500-square-meter specialty store in Beijing selling Chinese brands of the classic, casual, and modern styles: a total of 16 series of latest stylish products.

Competition with Domestic Capital Goods Makers Is Getting Really Tough

In the capital goods sector, competition is no less fierce.

For instance, within the five years up to 2006, domestic firms' share of China's $60 billion electrical equipment market, comprising automation and power-generation devices, increased from 55 percent to 65 percent. Their sales are growing twice as fast as the domestic market for electrical equipment as a whole. Currently, they are especially strong in the midrange segment. New powerful domestic competitors are emerging like Chint, a maker of low-voltage electronics, and Shanghai Electric, a manufacturer of power-generation equipment (McKinsey 2006). As time goes by, they are pursuing a high-end niche more and more. How should Western firms react?

Jack Perkowski, an American entrepreneur who recently started JFP Holdings, a merchant bank for China, and the author of the book *Managing the Dragon*, gives a very interesting example. One of his American clients makes electrical testers in the United States that can test for up to eight to nine items and sells them in China. Its competitors are GE and other world-famous electrical brands. About 15 Chinese manufacturers produce similar lower-end products, which can test only two to three items. The Chinese market for the latter is bigger than for eight-to nine-item testers. In a few years Chinese companies are expected to be making eight-to nine-item testers at a lower cost.

The question is: What can the U.S. producer do?

J. Perkowski suggests that it can and should start making two-to three-item testers in China, bringing in Chinese managers and workers—in other words, to become a full-fledged Chinese player (Harris 2010). This is the option two we discussed earlier. Definitely, at the company level such business strategy has its rationale. For instance, DMG of Germany, the world's largest maker of machine tools, is doing exactly what J. Perkowski recommends: It has started to develop low-cost models for Chinese customers and to produce them locally (Shintaku 2010).

Yet developments of this kind, while strengthening the production base of China, are weakening the bases of America, Europe, and Japan, accelerating production power shift (recollect the quote from H. Gai).

Tomorrow Chinese firms will be able to produce many high-end products of today, and will make them cheaper than their Western counterparts. If the West wants to preserve its production base, it will still have to enable domestic, not Chinese-based, factories of its firms to differentiate their products, further upgrade technologies, and raise the degree of sophistication. The governments have to aggressively promote the exports of those products to China and other emerging market countries. Also, much more attention has to be paid to development of products tailored to the needs of Chinese customers.

Thus, the problem posed by J. Perkowski, perhaps, may have one more solution: run ahead, develop even more high-end testers, produce them at home, and work to create the market for them in China, or, if this is not feasible, use your technological skills to develop, produce, and export similar high-end items.

The competition in the Chinese market is going to be very tough, but the fight for it is worthwhile. The West has to increase the number of domestic factories that can be strong fighters.

Chapter 7

Global Services Market: The West's Edge and China as Number Five

C hina's sensational performance as a manufacturing superpower left in the shadow its rapidly growing presence in the global market of commercial services. On the other hand, in the services sector the West retains a significant edge it can sharpen even further. Here it is in a good position to capture the rapidly expanding markets of China and other large developing countries, but at this point its services exports to those countries are surprisingly small.

China Joins the Ranks of Leading Services Exporters, but the United States Is Far Ahead

Between 2000 and 2009, China jumped from the eleventh to the fifth position among the world's largest services exporters, overtaking a number of European countries and Japan, and increasing its share of global services exports from 2 percent to almost 4 percent (Table 7.1).

Within the same period, its services exports grew 4.3 times against 2.3 times for the world, 2.8 times for Germany, 2.3 times for Spain, 1.9 times for the Netherlands and South Korea, 1.8 times for Japan and Italy, and 1.7 times for the United States and France.

India, whose services exports grew 5.5 times, was the fastest runner. Its share of the global services exports rose from 1.1 percent to 2.6 percent. Yet, the conventional view that while China is getting stronger in manufacturing, India is running ahead in services, is inaccurate. India's overall exports of services amount to no more than 58 percent of those of China.

As of 2009, China's services exports accounted for only 27.1 percent of those of the United States, and a little more than half those of the UK and Germany. If the 2000–2009 dynamics are preserved in 2010–2018, by the end of this period China will become the second-largest services exporter after the United States, its exports volume reaching a little less than 70 percent of America's.

Between 2000 and 2009, China reached the fastest annual growth rate for exports of transportation services: 23 percent, closely followed by India with 21 percent. Exports from the United States were growing

Table 7.1 Exports of Commercial Services by Country ($ million)

Country	2000	2009
United States	278,089	473,899
UK	118,567	233,316
Germany	79,659	226,638
France	82,115	142,487
China	30,146	128,600
Japan	69,430	125,858
Spain	52,112	122,126
Italy	59,898	101,237
India	16,031	87,434
World	1,483,900	3,350,200

SOURCE: WTO International Trade Statistics.

4 percent and from the 27 EU countries 9 percent a year. In 2009, China's exports in this sector reached $23.6 billion (3.4 percent of the world's total), and India's $10.8 billion (1.5 percent). The U.S. exports were $71.8 billion (10.2 percent), and extra-EU exports of the 27 EU countries $153.2 billion (21.9 percent).

Exports of China's *travel services* were growing 10 percent a year reaching $39.7 billion in 2009 (4.6 percent of the world's total) against 13 percent and $10.6 billion for India (1.2 percent of the world's total). The annual growth of EU exports was 8 percent and the United States 2 percent. In 2009, America's exports hit $120.3 billion, or 13.8 percent of the world's total, and the EU member states $95.4 billion and 10.9 percent.

So, even in the transportation and especially travel services, the sectors where China achieved most is still significantly lagging behind the Western powers. The latter continue to command global markets. Growth of India's exports of those services was remarkable, but in absolute terms they remain minor.

In the *financial* and *telecom services* sectors, China's global presence is almost invisible: It is not among the top 15 exporters (here and in the following, the EU is counted as a single exporter). India, at number seven, accounted for 1.9 percent of global exports of telecom services. Its share of the global financial services market was 1.4 percent. In the latter sector it is about to catch up with Japan (1.9 percent of the world's total), though remaining far behind the United States (21.1 percent) and the EU (25.6 percent).

The only sector where Western countries are not leading is *computer and information* services. Here India has established itself as the champion. In 2008, its exports reached $36,041 million and accounted for 19.4 percent of the world's total, which is about three times as much as the exports from the United States ($12,599 million and 6.8 percent respectively). Total EU exports were $42,500 million (22.8 percent). China was the fifth-largest exporter with $6,252 million and 3.4 percent respectively.

China's Trade Deficit

In its commercial services trade, India maintains a small surplus (Tables 7.1 and 7.2).

Table 7.2   Imports of Commercial Services by Country ($ million)

Country	2000	2009
United States	207,880	330,590
Germany	135,812	253,110
UK	96,893	160,873
China	35,858	158,200
Japan	105,230	146,903
France	64,400	126,425
Italy	54,632	114,581
Ireland		103,449
India		78,774
World	1,460,500	81,352

SOURCE: WTO International Trade Statistics.

China's services trade is in deficit. Contrary to merchandise trade, its imports of services are growing even faster than exports. In 2009, it was the world's fourth-largest services importer almost catching up with the UK, which was at number three. Also, it has become the largest net importer of services overtaking Germany and Japan. In 2009, China's net services imports reached $29,600 million (up from $5,712 million in 2000), Germany's $26,472 million, and Japan's $21,047 million.

On the other hand, the United States and the United Kingdom have noticeably strengthened their position as the major services trade surplus nations. Between 2000 and 2009, the United States effectively doubled its surplus from $70,209 million to $143,309 million, and the United Kingdom expanded it almost 3.5 times from $21,674 million to $72,443 million. France and Spain also maintain permanent and significant surpluses.

Overall, as far as the nations' trade balances are concerned, the picture in the services sector is almost the opposite of the one in the merchandise trade. In services, the West has a significant competitive edge versus China and is in a good position to establish a much wider presence in the Chinese market.

China Has a Structural Weakness in Services That Is Difficult to Overcome

China's weakness in services is of a structural character. It has its historical and cultural roots, especially the legacy of the several decades long epoch of Soviet-style socialism.

The mentality of many Chinese service companies and workers still does not match (if not runs contrary to) the very basic concept of services assuming that their provider should treat the customer like "a king," be extremely polite, attentive and reactive, and do everything he or she can to meet the customer's demands or requests. Though China's services exports are growing, the lack of the service tradition, low commitment of workers, poor management and shortage of experienced and well-trained personnel, especially high-skilled specialists capable of providing high-end professional services, make the overall picture of its service industry quite gloomy. It would be safe to say that consumers, both domestic and international, are not that happy about the "average" level of services provided by Chinese airline and railway companies, catering spots, hotels, travel agencies, recreation facilities, and so on. As local consumers' demand for a variety of good services is increasing, American, European and Japanese service providers have a good chance to exploit their competitive advantage in this area, establishing a stronger position at the Chinese market.

Here, however, comes a surprise. You may expect that, in the wake of what was written earlier, America and Europe are enjoying substantial surpluses in their services trade with China, not incomparable to their huge deficits in merchandise trade. But it is not so.

The U.S. and EU Surpluses in the Services Trade with China Are Meager

According to the Chinese statistical source, in 2008 EU-27's exports of services to China were $23,560 million, and imports $21,340 million. The U.S. services exports to China were $23,520 million and imports $22,790 million. In other words, the trade in services between China and the West was almost in equilibrium (National Bureau of Statistics 2010).

The U.S. and EU data are somewhat different. The EU services exports to China for the same year were estimated at $29,303 million, and imports at $21,977 million. For the U.S.-China trade the figures were $15,645 million and $9,825 million respectively. Nevertheless, according to the Western data too, surpluses were negligible: around $7 billion for the EU and $4 billion for the United States. (The same year, the EU's deficit in merchandise trade with China was $219 billion and America's $227 billion.)

China's share of the U.S. total services exports was just 3.0 percent. America's surplus was generated first and most by its trade with the EU, Canada, Japan, and Mexico. The share of China in the extra-EU services exports of the EU was even lower: 1.6 percent.

China's deficit was created first and most by its trade with Japan, South Korea, and other Asian countries.

The interim conclusion is very simple: America's and Europe's exports of services to China are too small, there is a lot of room to expand them, and on their part it would be unwise to miss the golden opportunity they have as the world's leading services nations.

By the way, it also applies to their services trade with India. The latter accounts for only 0.7 percent of the services exports from the EU and 2 percent from the United States.

The Right Time to Capture the Chinese Market

As trade items, services are not at all less important than goods. Furthermore, in relative terms they are getting increasingly important as global trade in services is growing faster than trade in goods: Average annual growth rates for 2000–2009 were respectively 9 percent and 8 percent. In 2009, global merchandise exports amounted to $12,490 billion, and global exports of services $3,350 billion (WTO 2010).

More emphasis on sharpening the West's competitive edge in this sector would not in any way mean that America and Europe are accepting the role of a services "appendage" to China. On the contrary, it could help them to enhance the lead in the fastest growing sector of the global economy having the greatest potential for the expansion of demand in the future. For America and Europe and, maybe, also Japan, time is ripe to use their edge in full to conquer the Chinese services market, still largely underdeveloped.

In this regard, a combination of three factors is working in favor of Western service providers. First, in today's China, the level of development and penetration of most services is low. Second, Chinese consumers' awareness about various kinds of services and their importance is growing. Third, contrary to manufacturing, Chinese domestic service companies are relatively weak.

Let us pick up the insurance industry as just one of the examples.

Life insurance penetration (total insurance premium income as percent of the GDP) in China in 2009 stood at 3.4 percent against the 7 percent world average (Xia 2011), and non-life insurance penetration in 2008 at 0.8 percent (Insurance review 2009) as opposed, for instance, to the OECD average of 3.6 percent (OECD 2011).

As domestic public and private institutions do not provide a sufficient level of protection against accident, disease, disability and death, as well as against the risks associated with unemployment and retirement, Chinese families are boosting their low-yield bank deposits to have money at hand for the "rainy day." Around 72 percent of all personal financial assets are held in cash and deposits (McKinsey 2009b). On the other hand, as time goes by and consumers' education progresses, more and more people come to understand the advantages of being insured, especially the fact that long-term insurance products can help them address the risks mentioned in a much more efficient way, freeing significant funds for consumption activities.

The Chinese government is gradually pursuing deregulation and improving the regulatory framework. Steps are made to promote insurance services in the vast countryside. The industry's growth rates are remarkably high even by Chinese standards. For instance, between 2005 and 2008, the life insurance industry is estimated to have grown almost 35 percent annually (McKinsey 2009b). The forecasts say that between 2011 and 2014, annual growth of all insurance premiums will be about 24 percent (Market Research 2011).

Yet, the total assets of China's insurance sector as of the middle of 2010, amounted to 4.57 trillion yuan, or $672 billion (*China Daily* 2010), which is comparable to the assets of just one major insurance company in the West, like Germany's Allianz, Italy's Generali Group or Japan's Nippon Life Insurance (around $600 billion each). Chinese insurers are still too small to catch up with the surging domestic demand.[1]

Thus, for services exporters it is the right time to start moving, and for Western governments to press Beijing harder to open up its services market. Don't be late.

Note

1. In India the situation is largely similar. Life insurance penetration as of 2009 was 4.2 percent and non-life insurance penetration only 0.6 percent. Average growth in the life insurance sector (first year premiums) between the 2002–2003 and 2009–2010 fiscal years averaged 23 percent. In the non-life insurance sector, annual growth between the 2007–2008 and 2009–2010 fiscal years was 10.3 percent (Insurance Regulatory and Development Authority 2011). About 70 percent of the population is not covered by any kind of insurance (Insurance review 2009). Total assets of the state-owned Life Insurance Corporation of India, the dominant player in the industry and the country's largest investor, are about $170 billion (Govt Vacancies 2010).

Chapter 8

Is China a New Financial Superpower?

C hina's growing production and export power enhances its financial strength as well. This is natural. However, compared to its sensational emergence as a leading manufacturing and trading nation, the process of its ascending to the position of a major financial power is more fragmentary and complicated.

China's Overseas Assets

China has by far the largest foreign exchange reserves in the world, about three times as large as Japan, which is number two. It is also rapidly emerging as the leading international lender. In contrast, China's role as a foreign direct and portfolio investor is still considerably smaller than that of America, major European countries, and Japan.

For the time being, the story of China's growing financial clout is, first and foremost, the story of the unprecedented increase of the financial power of the Chinese state.

As of the end of 2010, China's total overseas gross financial assets were estimated at $4,126 billion. Its major portion: $2,914.2 billion or 71 percent, was accounted for by foreign exchange reserves, compared to $310.8 billion or 7 percent for the outstanding balance of outward foreign direct investment (FDI); $257.1 billion or 6 percent for portfolio investment, and $643.9 billion or 16 percent for other foreign investment: mainly financial and trade loans, and deposits (Searchina 2011).

Due to its exceptionally high foreign reserves, as of the end of 2010, China's total *net* foreign assets (gross foreign assets less gross foreign liabilities) have become the second-largest in the world after Japan's: $1,791 billion (Searchina 2011) and $3,085 billion (Ministry of Finance Japan 2011) respectively. For comparison, Germany's net foreign assets were about $1,049 billion (Bundesbank 2011), and the United States had negative foreign assets of minus $2,865.8 billion as its gross foreign liabilities are larger than its assets (Bureau of Economic Analysis 2011b). So, technically today China is the world's second-largest net creditor nation.

On the contrary, its *gross* foreign assets are much smaller than those of the United States: $4,126 billion and $18,379 billion respectively. They are also considerably smaller than Japan's (about $6.9 trillion) and Germany's (about $7.2 trillion).

$3 Trillion-Plus Foreign Reserves: Implications for China and for the West

In March 2011, China's foreign exchange reserves exceeded the $3 trillion mark.

This tremendous amount stems from the status of the country's balance of payments. Maintaining a huge foreign trade surplus and, consequently, a current account surplus, it also has a comfortable and usually quite substantial surplus in the capital and financial account, as foreigners invest in China much more than the Chinese overseas (in most countries the current account balance and the capital and financial account balance have opposite signs, which means that the current account surplus is somewhat offset by the capital account deficit or vice versa).

Unprecedented growth of China's foreign reserves has two major implications for the West and for the whole world.

The most important one is Beijing's position as the largest foreign creditor of the American government. China holds about 14 percent of all U.S. Treasury Bonds. Whether one likes it or not, it gives the Chinese government a strong leverage to push its interests on a wide range of economic, political, and security issues. Currently, China's role as a creditor is becoming increasingly noticeable on the European continent as well, and will apparently increase further as public debt problems in a growing number of the EU countries are becoming critical.

The second implication is China's ability to pursue foreign acquisitions and other strategic overseas investment in a buy-whatever-the-price fashion. In other words, the Chinese buy foreign assets they consider important even when their prices reach the levels that would be prohibitive for a private Western investor. While Western governments can block transactions of this kind in their own countries, and they often do, they can do little to prevent China from using its foreign reserves as a tool to boost its political and economic clout in the Third World. We will explore this issue more in detail later on.

On the other hand, soaring foreign reserves are posing challenges for China itself. The central bank governor Zhou Xiaochuan is clearly saying that foreign reserves have exceeded the reasonable level and are becoming difficult to manage (Schneider 2011).

In 2006, the China Investment Corporation (CIC) was established to manage a very small portion of the total: $200 billion. Today it is the largest Sovereign Wealth Fund in the world.

However, it is often noted that, overall, the reserves could be managed in a much more efficient manner and bring higher returns. The yields from U.S. Treasury bonds are very low. Some other investments, like the one into Merrill Lynch, ended in a substantial loss.

Next, also on the negative side, a dramatic increase of foreign reserves is accompanied by rising inflationary pressures. The reason is that, basically, the foreign currency accumulating in the People's Bank of China is exchanged for the national currency, which is injected into the national economy. It amplifies inflationary trends and elevates the risk of an asset bubble. (Inflationary pressures are significantly increasing also due to soaring global prices for food, fuel, and mineral resources, and the legacy of the 4 trillion yuan economic stimulus of 2008.) There is a risk of a chain reaction of the increase of foreign reserves, growing liquidity injections into the economy, rising inflation, monetary policy tightening, and the fall of economic growth rates.

To sterilize dollars, the central bank makes the country's major banks turn over their foreign exchange in return for its interest-bearing securities. The scale of such sterilization may exceed $12 billion a week. It helps to contain inflationary trends, but locks up capital, as this money cannot be lent or invested (Schneider 2011).

To tackle the excessive liquidity injection problem, China needs much larger outflows of capital (see further on). In other words, the Chinese have to invest much more overseas. It could also open new business opportunities for domestic companies, financial institutions, and individual investors.

The Chinese government has introduced some policy measures supporting outbound investment, but they are still too weak and fragmentary, while restrictions are still strong. Also, it is often argued that it is not relevant for China as a developing country to export much capital.

In our view, for China with its exceptionally large foreign exchange reserves this is not necessarily the case. However, it cannot be denied that the key issue is whether or not these reserves can be used more actively and efficiently for the country's own development.

Though some attempts in this direction have been made, the situation remains unclear.

For instance, the Finance Ministry bought $106 billion of foreign currency from the central bank and used it for the recapitalization of the Big Four banks and the Development Bank of China. However, it turned out to be only an accounting detour, as, after all, the central bank repurchased the foreign exchange involved (Truman 2010).

In a new development, the CIC has announced plans to invest the foreign exchange it manages into the shares of Chinese companies listed overseas in order to boost technologically intensive industries.

Nevertheless, it would be safe to say that the accumulation of such huge foreign reserves by a country where many regions are still underdeveloped and a lot of people live below poverty level looks somewhat unnatural. Basically, countries with large foreign reserves are in the best position to become major international donors. However, China is a developing country itself. Thus, logically, it looks relevant to utilize part of its reserves, which after all manifest the state's wealth, for official development assistance to its own provinces, villages, and townships to build infrastructure and houses for the poor, protect environment, improve livelihood, and so on. The problem lies in the monetary field: You cannot use accumulated foreign currencies directly for investing in projects at home.

However, apparently, Beijing would not turn down proposals about development aid for the purposes mentioned if they came from overseas (and, actually, it still gets some development funding from the World Bank, the Asian Development Bank, and so on). Today there cannot be too many proposals of this kind because China itself has a lot of foreign currency, but perhaps the Chinese government could use some of the foreign reserves for "domestic official development aid" for imports of the equipment, materials, services, and so on needed to launch development and livelihood improvement projects in the country's less-developed regions.

This could ease the financial burden of provincial administrations whose debts are beginning to cause concern, and also contribute to balancing the trade between China and its Western counterparts in a way that is beneficial for both sides. After all, it is quite simple: The West has a lot of things to sell to China that could make the life of the Chinese people, especially poor people, better, and the Chinese government has the money to buy them. Only political will and a bit of creativity and imagination are needed to make it a win-win game.

China Has Become the Largest International Lender for Developing Countries

China is rapidly emerging as one of the world's leading lender nations.

At the end of the previous decade it became the largest international lender for developing countries, surpassing the World Bank. According to the research by the *Financial Times*, in 2009–2010 the

China Development Bank and China Export–Import Bank extended loans of at least $110 billion, while the World Bank's loans between mid-2008 and mid-2010 hit its own record of $100.3 billion (Dyer, Anderlin, and Sender 2011).

In terms of assets, Chinese commercial banks, especially the Big Four (Industrial and Commercial Bank of China, Bank of China, China Construction Bank, and Agricultural Bank of China), are rapidly approaching the world's top 10.

In 2010, the Industrial and Commercial Bank of China rose to the eleventh position in the world with assets of $1,726 billion, which almost equaled those of Citigroup ($1,857 billion) and comprised 58.2 percent of the assets of the leader, France's BNP Paribas: $2,965 billion (Alexander 2011).

Chinese commercial banks are becoming increasingly important lenders for Western companies.

China's Outbound Foreign Investment: Accelerating, but the Lag Remains

Until recently, China was not on the list of the world's major foreign direct investor nations. An important breakthrough came in 2008. According to the National Bureau of Statistics, outbound FDI increased dramatically to $55,907 million from $26,506 million in the previous year (flow; FDI by financial institutions is not included). In 2009, it rose further to $56,529 million (National Bureau of Statistics 2010) and in 2010, according to the Commerce Ministry of China, it hit $59 billion.

In 2009, China entered the list of the world's top five foreign direct investor countries, but the scale of its FDI was only about one-seventh that of the United States, one-third of France, and two-thirds of Japan (Table 8.1).

The gap will turn even more significant if we take into account that Chinese FDI remains biased toward Hong Kong, which in 2009 accounted for as much as $35,601 billion or 63.0 percent of the total. It was followed by the Cayman Islands ($5,366 million and 9.5 percent respectively). The next-most-important recipient was Australia

Table 8.1 Outbound Foreign Direct Investment by Country ($ millions)

	2008	2009
United States	330,491	248,074
France	161,071	147,161
Germany	134,592	62,705
UK	161,056	18,463
Japan	128,019	74,699
China★	52,150	48,000
Italy	43,839	43,918
Russia	56,091	46,057
World	1,928,799	1,100,933

★Data for China differs slightly from the one presented by the Chinese National Bureau of Statistics.
SOURCE: UNCTAD. World Investment Report 2010.

($2,436 million and 4.3 percent)—first of all, its mining industry. The FDI to all European countries combined (including Russia, which was the largest recipient) was $3,353 million and 5.9 percent and to the United States $908 million and 1.6 percent (National Bureau of Statistics 2010).

So, overall, if you exclude the FDI to Hong Kong, China's total outbound FDI would be around $20 billion, which means that, in spite of the recent gains, its role as a foreign direct investor nation remains very limited—even though Chinese acquisitions of well-known Western companies have become a hot topic around the world.

Acquisitions account for around 40 percent of China's total FDI. The major targets are mining industry, high-tech manufacturing firms, and well-known but usually ailing companies possessing famous brands. Such acquisitions are usually carried out with the backing of the government, mostly by state-owned companies.

On the other hand, Chinese companies, especially the private ones, are gradually increasing FDI of quite a conventional character. They are investing in India, North Korea, Vietnam, Myanmar, and elsewhere in the developing world seeking lower production costs or better access to local markets. Also, more and more often, they are coming to the West entirely on their own initiative (without the government's backing), attracted by markets, technologies, and high-skilled human resources. In these cases Chinese investors act basically the same way and pursue the same goals as investors from any other country, whether America, a European state, or Japan.

China's overseas portfolio investment is also noticeably increasing.

In 2009 it was $57.0 billion—almost three times as much as in 2000: $20.7 billion (National Bureau of Statistics 2010), but still significantly smaller than America's $208.2 billion (U.S. Census Bureau 2011a) and Japan's $170.0 billion (Ministry of Internal Affairs and Communications 2011) or Germany's 148.7 billion euro (Bundesbank 2010).

Chinese Households' Financial Assets: Still Tiny

In relative terms, the Chinese save much more than Westerners. It is a well-known and frequently mentioned fact. In the 2000s, households' net savings in China stood at 20–25 percent of their disposable income (Wang & Wen 2011). As for major Western economies, in 2008 the ratio was 11.6 percent in France, 11.2 percent in Germany, 8.6 percent in Italy, 2.7 percent in the United States, and minus 4.5 percent in the United Kingdom. The average for the EU-27 was 5.8 percent. In Japan, as of 2007, the net savings rate was 3.8 percent (OECD 2010). (We will discuss Western countries' savings more in detail in Part Two.)

Much less frequently mentioned is the fact that in absolute terms, total families' savings in China are still considerably smaller than in the United States or Japan.

As of the end of 2009, Chinese households were estimated to hold around 26,077 billion yuan, or about $3,818 billion (National Bureau of Statistics 2010) in their savings accounts as opposed to $6,130 billion held by American households (U.S. Census Bureau 2011a).

Overall, according to the latest estimates of the Daiwa Institute of Research, households' total gross financial assets in China have exceeded $5 trillion (DIR 2010), which is still not comparable with America's $45.5 trillion as of the end of the first quarter of 2010 (the data for the United States includes financial assets of nonprofit organizations).

Table 8.2   Households' Financial Assets (end of 2009)

	Total ($ billion)	Per Capita ($)
United States	41,591	132,178
Japan	14,643	115,159
Germany	6,068	73,850
UK	6,065	98,511
France	4,975	79,801
Italy	4,576	76,434
China	4,407	3,769

SOURCE: Allianz Global Wealth Report 2010.

Comparative cross-country data for the end of 2009 is presented in Table 8.2.

By the absolute amount of households' financial assets, China stood only at number seven, its total comprising a little more than one-tenth that of the United States and a little less than one-third of Japan. As for the financial assets per capita, Chinese families' average wealth accounts for only about one-twentieth to one-thirtieth of that of the households in the developed countries.

At this point China's strength as a global financial power does not stem from the wealth accumulated by Chinese people. It is rather the opposite: State coffers overfilled with cash on the one hand and mostly not-so-wealthy, if not poor, households on the other. This situation may be socially explosive.

Is China a New Financial Superpower? Yes and No

Is China already a new major financial power? Yes, definitely yes. However, it is a financial superpower of a very special kind.

Its financial strength does not stem from the wealth of the vast majority of its citizens. First and foremost, it reflects the might of the state, which, due to soaring exports and inward investment, accumulated a tremendous amount of foreign currency reserves.

The Chinese ruling elite feels very comfortable on the international arena using this financial might as big leverage to win concessions from its counterparts and push its own interests and priorities.

This is one of the major reasons why it is not that eager to reduce the country's trade surplus and to speed up the appreciation of yuan. The weak yuan is a political choice whose main goal is to strengthen the system of Communist Party rule.

China is rapidly emerging as a leading international lender. Its major state-owned banks are feeling more and more confident as major players in the global banking community.

In other important respects—effectively all the respects unrelated to the state and state-owned financial entities—today's China is not a financial superpower in the true meaning of the word.

The role of its companies (not to say its individuals) as international investors remains comparatively small, though it is growing. Most companies are still lacking international experience and expertise. Besides, for many of them incentives to go abroad often appear to be weak as there is a lot of investment opportunity at home.

China's domestic financial market is heavily regulated and offers only a narrow range of financial instruments. The country does not play any noticeable role as an exporter of financial services either. With the exception of bank lending, their global market is dominated by the West, and there are no noticeable signs of Chinese financial institutions being ready to join the leaders' ranks.

Demand for the yuan as an international currency remains comparatively small, and the probability of it playing the role comparable to that of the dollar or the euro in the foreseeable future is close to none.

In the coming decade, Western governments, starting from the United States, will become increasingly dependent on China as a creditor. Chinese state-owned banks will establish a key position among the world's major lenders to clients not only in the developing, but also in the developed world. A relatively narrow circle of big companies, especially state-owned ones, will rapidly develop as important foreign direct investors.

On the other hand, the formation of a wider range of strong Chinese multinationals, including private firms—a range comparable to the one in the major countries of the West—will take a longer period of time, as well as the emergence of a cohort of Chinese large-scale investors into securities around the world. In these areas, competition from China is still relatively weak.

Conclusions

First, China's nominal GDP has just become the second largest in the world. From now on, the world economy will be rapidly adopting a two-towers-dominated shape: with the United States and Chinese towers much taller than all other buildings. Moreover, the Chinese tower will continue growing much faster than the American and overtake it, most likely, in the first half of this century.

Within this U.S.-China duopoly, China will first of all further strengthen its position as the leading manufacturing nation, while America will be the number one services nation. At the same time, China will be gradually becoming a stronger competitor in services as well. On their part, America and the West have opportunities in manufacturing, but will have to work hard not to miss them.

Second, "China as the number one producer" has become an international standard for most manufacturing industries and products. As a rule, gaps between China and the followers are increasing. The circle of industries and goods whose top producer is another nation (in most cases, it is the United States) is becoming more and more narrow. By and large, it is already limited to several materials-producing sectors.

Third, China's drive to the number one position in merchandise exports, mostly in manufacturing, was even faster than in manufacturing production. In the electronics/electrical products and the light industry consumer goods sectors it is becoming not just a leading, but a dominant exporter. However, in other industries, China's growing lead in production does not necessarily translate into the lead in exports, as most of its production increment is absorbed by the domestic market. In these industries China often emerges as a big net importer. Especially, growth of China's manufacturing production and exports is accompanied by a rapid increase of the imports of production inputs. The key point is what countries and companies will succeed in tapping China's capital goods market. Up till now, in this regard East Asia has been doing much better than the West.

Fourth, Chinese producers have become the world's dominant players in the production and exports of low-tech–low-end–mass products and are rapidly expanding their presence in the high-tech–low-end–mass products segment. Their global presence in the low-end–differentiated-products segment and especially in the high-end products segments is much weaker, though increasing. At the domestic market they are rapidly occupying the latter two niches as well.

Fifth, China's manufacturing production/export offensive drastically changes the global rules of the game and the status of Western manufacturers. For the West, it is getting increasingly difficult, if not meaningless, to protect traditional local industries from the inflow of cheap made-in-China products by imposing punitive tariffs or other import restrictions. The notion of local industry itself is changing.

Because China-West production cost differentials are enormous, Western factories are doomed to lose in the low-tech–low-end mass-products segment and, more and more, also in the segment of high-tech–low-end mass products. In these two segments, globalization and the Chinese offensive deprive them of the economic rationale to continue operating. It is a new globalized world, and it is high time to change the mentality. In a way, it is very simple. Here is the world—your world—and if you want to manufacturer a particular item, find the place in this world where you can make it most efficiently and the markets where it will sell well. If you stick to a different way of thinking and want, by all means, to produce in your home country (it is understandable: In spite of globalization, many people, perhaps the majority, would still prefer to live and work in their homeland), then you have to find an answer to the key question: What particular products does it make sense to manufacture there and why?

Basically, today's Western factories have no other rational option but to drift to the segments of low-end–differentiated products and, especially, high-end products—in other words, to aggressively differentiate their products raising nonprice competitiveness. This drive has to be accompanied by the increase in exports, especially to the most dynamic Chinese and other Third World markets. Governments have to do much more for exports promotion.

Exportability of the product—its acceptance by consumers around the world—is becoming the major criterion of whether or not it should be manufactured in this or that particular place.

The number of West-based manufacturers is and will be declining, and only "excellent producers" capable of differentiating their products and competing on their quality and uniqueness will feel good at home. Others will either have to move to China and the like to produce mass products or continue a bitter fight for survival.

Sixth, though China is becoming an increasingly important player in the global market of services as well, it is not a strong service economy. To become one, it lacks tradition, committed and skilled human resources, and know-how. Too many Chinese service workers still do not understand the basic concept of services just as the main hero of *Rainman*, brilliantly played by Dustin Hoffman, did not understand the concept of money. In the services sector the West has a substantial competitive edge, and it should not miss its chance. Currently, its exports of services to China are too small.

Seventh, China has become one of the world's leading financial powers and, technically, the number two creditor nation, but its financial might first and foremost reflects the strength of the Chinese state. The major manifestation of this strength is the unprecedented amount of foreign exchange reserves. They are working as a very important factor in global politics, letting China set terms on a wide range of issues. On the other hand, they are bringing very modest returns and are not used efficiently enough to solve China's development problems and raise the living standards of its people.

As far as household wealth is concerned, China is not, by far, a financial superpower. Though Chinese families' saving rates are exceptionally high, the absolute volume of their financial assets is still insignificant by international standards. China is a rich state with people who are far from rich.

Part Two

THE GLOBAL DOWNTURN
AND BEYOND:
WESTERN CAPITALISM
AND CHINESE CAPITALISM

T he crisis of 2008–2009 had enormous repercussions for the global economic power balance. Effectively it was a farewell to the Western-led world. Though all major national economies were hit, in relative terms, China's position versus the United States, Europe, and Japan became as strong as never before in modern history.

Chapter 9

The Global Crisis Was Not Really Global

U sually it is called a global financial and economic crisis. However, it was not really global—at least because China, India,
and other large Asian economies, first of all Indonesia and
Vietnam, as well as a number of other large emerging economies (LEEs)
around the world, retained significant positive growth rates. Created by
the United States, it was first and foremost an American crisis, and then
a Western crisis.

The data vividly shows that in 2009 Western powers experienced
unusually deep GDP falls—the worst in the whole postwar period,
and so did small Asian countries highly dependent on Western export
markets. On the contrary, China-led large emerging economies of
Asia comprised a growing group (Table 9.1). The only exception
was Thailand, whose GDP fell, but this happened largely because of
domestic political turmoil. On Africa's part, for example, Nigeria
grew 7.0 percent, Tanzania 6.7 percent, and the Republic of Congo

Table 9.1   Real GDP Growth Rates in 2009 to 2010 (%)

	2009	2010
United States	−3.5	3.0
Japan	−6.3	4.0
Eurozone	−4.3	1.8
Germany	−5.1	3.6
France	−2.6	1.4
UK	−4.9	1.4
Taiwan	−1.9	10.9
Hong Kong	−2.7	7.0
Singapore	−0.8	14.5
Malaysia	−1.7	7.2
China	*9.2*	*10.3*
India	*6.8*	*10.1*
Indonesia	*4.6*	*6.1*
Vietnam	*5.3*	*6.8*
Philippines	*1.1*	*7.6*
Thailand	−2.3	7.8

SOURCES: IMF WEO International Database, September 2011; ADB, Asian Development Outlook 2011; National statistical agencies.

7.5 percent. In 2010, all Asian economies except Japan and a cohort of other large emerging economies accelerated to around 7 percent or more (for instance, Brazil and Turkey, which contracted in 2008, grew 7.5 percent and 8.2 percent respectively). In contrast, in the West, among the major economies, only Japan and Germany managed to jump above the 3 percent mark. Recovery remains slow, and there is still a lot to be done to cure various postcrisis economic diseases.

Though the epicenter of the shock lay in the banking and finance sector, the crisis was not purely financial. Behind it stood structural weaknesses of the U.S. and European economies, such as unsustainable consumption patterns and the flaws of corporate governance.

To get over it, along with tightening and expanding financial regulations, America and Europe will need painful structural adjustments, especially a severe restraint on public spending and a further trimming of the welfare state. These adjustments will squeeze economic growth and cause high social tensions.

In contrast, in the crisis years China and other LEEs proved capable of growing fast, even when Western economies were contracting. At the beginning of the new decade, they are in a good position to preserve strong growth dynamics if not to accelerate.

Western societies are frustrated by the poor performance of their developed and mature market economies. In the wake of the crisis, one of the most popular themes in America, Europe, and Japan was the failure of capitalism and the need to strengthen government intervention not only to put the economy back on track, but also in the long term.

China and other LEEs, on the contrary, are accommodating more and more elements of the classical, Anglo-Saxon–style market economy and amplifying market incentives for companies irrespective of their form of ownership. Conventional wisdom says that Chinese state capitalism is different from the Western capitalist system. However, in reality it was exactly marketization and partial Westernization that served as major systemic drivers of China's economic growth.

Chapter 10

Western Crisis:
Three Major Factors

The Western crisis of 2008–2009, the worst since the Great Depression, can be explained by three major factors.

Unaffordable Consumption
and Households Deeper in Debt

First, it was the crisis of consumption patterns and lifestyles. Many Western households had tiny savings and accumulated debts that were too big. Americans and Europeans have to ask themselves a simple, but very basic question: Are we living right? Are our lifestyles financially sustainable?

Not all Western countries are similar in this regard. The United States is the most typical example of biased and adventurous consumption. Countries like Germany and Switzerland represent another pole.

R. Weagley presents unique comparative data on the consumer finances in China and the United States (Weagley 2010). The data on China are based on the results of the survey of more than 2,000 urban Chinese households residing in class-one and class-two cities, conducted by the Tsinghua University.

Converted to dollars, the average annual household income of the Chinese families surveyed was $10,220 as opposed to the $84,300 average for U.S. households. In both China and the United States, the average family assets were about eight times its average income. However, the average U.S. household's debt comprised 136 percent of its income, while the average ratio for a Chinese family was no more than 17 percent.

Out of the Chinese families surveyed, 85 percent owned a home, but only 11 percent carried a mortgage on their property. In the United States, as of 2007, 69 percent of the families were homeowners, and 70 percent of the homeowners were carrying a debt on the property in the form of a mortgage or an equity loan. While in the United States mortgage debt is encouraged through a subsidy in tax code, China's policy is to provide housing without high indebtedness—through employer home purchase plans for employees and so on. Less than 1 percent of the Chinese use consumer loans to purchase consumer goods. In the United States, 47 percent of the families have installment loans and 46 percent carry a credit card balance (Weagley 2010).

Though China is cautiously encouraging a gradual expansion of consumer credit, it is clear that, as far as consumption patterns and lifestyles are concerned, the two economic giants represent two opposite cultures: of living on debt and of not living on debt. It is not difficult to say which one makes the economy more vulnerable.

A prudent household decides what and how much to consume depending on its income. Income comes first, setting reasonable consumption limits.

For many households in the West, starting from the United States, it is the reverse. First comes a consumption standard considered necessary to achieve or to maintain. If disposable income is not enough, borrowing increases up to the point where the standard is achievable. The standard itself depends not only on the personal requirements of every particular consumer, but also on the established perceptions of the consumption level relevant for a more or less well-to-do family: a house it should live in, a car it should ride, a set of durable goods it should have, and so on. You either meet this standard or lose the esteem of the people around you.

As time goes by, the standard is rising, often faster than the households' incomes. It is here that the financial crisis mechanism starts to unveil.

As the financial sector develops and offers a widening variety of lending schemes, households increasingly rely on loans, especially when interest rates are low. The lion's share of the loans they get is accounted for by mortgages. The range of borrowers expands as lower-income households, often with a poor credit record, join in. Lending risks increase, but as long as the economy is growing, asset prices are rising (and they rise faster as more and more buyers emerge, tempted by easy credit), and growth expectations remain high, financial institutions continue to increase lending to marginal borrowers seeking to boost their business and assuming that the loans will be returned or at least that the collateralized assets will shield them from losses. The trend grows stronger as more and more debts are securitized: Lenders feel more risk-averse as they can get their cash faster and risks are dispersed. However, at a certain point marginal borrowers start to default, which, together with the burst of the asset bubble, drives the financial sector into the crisis. Dispersing risks through securitization only widens the range of financial players suffering a blow.

Not only lenders, but also borrowers have to bear heavy responsibility for this kind of a crisis. The financial sector debacle, spurred by their irresponsible behavior, disables the national economy in general and also hits a heavy blow to the whole world if the national economy in question is large.

Time has come to realize that in today's globalized economy crazy lending-borrowing games played by the Western households wishing to have much more than they can afford, and by financial institutions driven by greed and ignoring the very basic rules of prudent lending, hit a karate-style blow to billions of people around the planet. The crazy borrowers' defaults and the crazy lenders' lumps of non-performing loans unleash a chain reaction of financial-sector agony, depression in the national economy, and finally the global downturn if the economy in question is large.

Table 10.1   Net Saving Rate in Household Disposable Income (%)

	2001	2002	2003	2004	2005	2006	2007	2008
United States	2.8	3.7	3.8	3.4	1.5	2.5	1.7	2.7
EU	7.5	7.4	7.3	6.6	6.4	5.8	5.5	5.8
UK	1.5	−0.1	0.4	−1.7	−1.3	−2.9	2.6	0.6
Germany	9.4	9.9	10.3	10.2	9.9	9.1	8.2	8.6
France	12.5	13.7	12.5	12.4	11.4	11.4	12.0	11.6
Italy	10.5	11.2	10.3	10.2	9.9	9.1	8.2	8.6
Spain	5.6	5.6	6.0	4.9	4.7	4.2	3.6	6.1
Netherlands	9.5	8.4	7.5	7.3	6.3	6.0	8.1	6.8
Japan	5.2	5.1	3.9	3.6	3.8	3.6	3.8	NA

SOURCE: OECD Factbook.

During the economic boom of the mid-2000s, in most industrially developed countries of the West saving rates were declining (Table 10.1), and household debts rising amid an increasing availability of credit. Not surprisingly, consumer spending was growing faster than households' disposable income.

In the United States, household saving rates had been decreasing for more than 20 years before they began elevating in 2008. As stocks and home prices were mostly going up, American families spent a growing portion of their incomes, reducing savings to near zero: In 2005–2007 saving rates experienced drops to a below 1 percent level (Feldstein 2009).

Seeking to consume more, many Americans and Europeans did not hesitate to borrow. By 2007, the households' leverage ratio (the ratio of household debt to disposable income) hit 199 percent in Denmark, 191 percent in Ireland, 185 percent in the Netherlands, 143 percent in Italy, and 130 percent in the United States. Countries with comparatively low indebtedness included France (60 percent), Belgium (64 percent), and Germany (82 percent) (Glick and Lansing 2010).

Between 1997 and 2007, the ratio soared 85 percentage points in Ireland, 82 points in the Netherlands, 69 points in Denmark, 65 points in Portugal, 52 points in Spain, 50 points in Norway, and 42 points in the United States. In Austria it rose 13 points, in Belgium 14 points, in France 15 points, and in Germany and Japan it fell 2 points and 5 points respectively. The larger the leverage, the greater was the private consumption plunge in the crisis years (Glick and Lansing 2010).

The U.S. subprime loans disaster, the starting point of the crisis, was caused not only by Freddie, Fannie, and the like, but also by American households whose incomes and purchasing power were too modest compared to excessively high standards they set for their homes. The problem worsened as the rise of the number of home buyers caused by easy access to credit pushed house prices further up at the same time, to unprecedented highs against disposable incomes.

G. Amronin and A. Paulson estimated that, with the third quarter of 2008 as a starting point, total losses from subprime loans in the United States would reach $364 billion, "in addition" to around $133 billion losses from prime loans. It was a default tsunami. The percentage of subprime loans that had defaulted (60 days or more overdue 12 months after the loan was made) was 14.6 percent for loans made in 2006, and 20.5 percent for loans extended in 2007. For comparison, the share of defaulted mortgages for loans originated in 2002 and 2003 was less than 7 percent (Amronin and Paulson 2009).

According to the rules of the market economy, or just fairness, defaulted borrowers have to take responsibility for their failure. At least they have neither economic prerequisites nor the moral right to live in the houses they pledged to but failed to pay for. Foreclosures are a highly natural, fair and probably minimal penalty, even though in the aftermath of the crisis they constrain growth and slow down a long-awaited recovery.

In broader terms, the crisis showed that many Westerners are not at all as rich as they want to be, as they pretend to be, and as they seemed to be to people in other parts of the world. You've got to be more modest, guys!

Gambling Capitalism

Second, the crisis of 2008–2009 was caused by a dramatic rise in the volume of transactions with structured financial products. More and more, Western capitalism was turning into gambling capitalism.

For investors, structured financial products provide a wide range of options regarding risks and returns. When you buy an ordinary bond, periodic coupons are attached to receive regular interest payments, and at the maturity date you are paid the final principle. When you buy a corporate stock, you are paid dividends. In both cases your payoffs are derived from the cash flow of the issuer itself. When you buy a structured product, it is not so: The payoffs are linked to the performance of one or more underlying assets the issuer has chosen.

Investments in conventional stocks and bonds are based on the investors' assessment of the present performance and future prospects of a particular business organization. Investments in structured financial instruments are more of a game, or gambling. The more complex the instruments are, the more difficult it is to properly assess and predict the performance of all the assets involved and to calculate the risks associated with them. To win this game, you have to be somewhat like a gambler: shrewd, imaginative, but also lucky. In the good times, with a little bit of luck, you make enormous profits and feel like a king. When luck says good-bye, you are down on the ground.

The structured products in the center of the financial crisis story were collateralized debt obligations (CDO) based on subprime mortgages. It is a type of structured asset-based security whose value and payments are derived from a portfolio of fixed-income underlying assets. The first CDO is said to have been issued back in 1987 in Britain by bankers at the now-defunct Drexel Burnham Lambert. In 20 years the size of their market reached $2 trillion, but a real boom started in 2004 and ended in 2007 (Treanor 2008).

Issued by major investment banks and given high ratings by leading credit rating agencies, they were actively bought by banks, insurance companies, mutual funds, and other investors attracted by very high returns. In 2007, when subprime borrowers started to default, they began to blow up, sending shock waves across financial markets around the world. In April 2009, the IMF estimated that toxic assets held by banks and other financial institutions, mostly in the developed countries, could reach $4 trillion posing the threat of systemic failures in the banking system (IMF 2009a). Six months later it changed the estimate to about $3.4 trillion (IMF 2009b).

The CDO debacle and the subprime loans fiasco amplified one another.

While luck was on hand, returns on CDO investments soared, bringing with it an abundance of cash. It weakened incentives for prudent management of financial institutions. Lending criteria were loosened, loans being extended to millions of American and other households with poor credit histories. They would not have been extended if banks had not been so confident and risk-averse due to the inflow of money from the transactions with subprime mortgages–based CDO.

Such overlending only increased the pain when subprime borrowers defaulted and the CDO market collapsed.

The Failure of State Regulation, Corporate Governance, and Business Morality

Third, the crisis occurred because no one—neither the state, nor top managers, nor shareholders—put the transactions with tricky financial instruments under proper control before it was too late. Financiers entrusted to carry out those transactions eventually got a free hand, made unbelievably big money and, finally, overdid it.

In January 2002, Sir Howard Davies, then the chairman of the Financial Services Authority (FSA), made an interesting confession: "One investment banker recently described synthetic CDO to me as the most toxic element of the financial markets today. When an investment banker talks of toxicity, a regulator is bound to take a heightened interest" (Treanor 2008). Bound to, but apparently didn't. The transactions in question remained out of the regulators' sight. The state failed to fulfill the major role it has to play in the market economy: setting the rules for doing business and enforcing businesspeople to comply.

This was Western capitalism's major structural failure.

Six years later, when he was already the director of the London School of Economics, Sir Howard discussed the issue with the *Guardian*. According to the newspaper, "the distilled version is that insurance companies were buying products they did not understand because they were attracted by the higher returns on offer. Little attention was paid to any potential risk because the rewards were so attractive." He defined the CDO buyers as "naïve capital" (Treanor 2008).

There is a Russian proverb saying that sometimes "naivety is worse than robbery." If Sir Howard's definition applies, this was definitely the case.

The CDO buyers who didn't bother to understand the product, and to assess risks, were not limited to insurance companies, but, as mentioned, included banks, investment funds, and other financial institutions as well as nonfinancial corporations. Risk models created and used by banks to meet regulatory requirements did not identify CDO as risky instruments (Treanor 2008).

Didn't know, didn't care, didn't do. . . . All these "technical" things, or rather, problems with basic work attitudes and the lack of responsibility on the part of people in charge, were, of course, a key part of the financial debacle story.

However, make just one step forward and again you will reach a structural dimension of the crisis: The CDO fiasco was also the result of the failure of the mechanisms of corporate governance.

The perception of a Western, namely Anglo-Saxon corporate system as shareholders' capitalism, meaning that shareholders exercise effective control over managers preventing the latter's too risky and irresponsible actions, proved to be a myth. In real life, it turned out to be exactly the opposite. Shareholders of leading financial institutions and a number of nonfinancial companies, which collapsed in 2008–2009 because of managers' adventurism, greed, or inability to find solutions for pressing problems, failed to stand up to protect their interests and to stop mismanagement.

In the failed financial institutions and companies, the shareholders' voices were unheard. Nonexecutive directors, who were supposed to protect their interests and exercise control over managers, were too agreeable and/or were not provided enough access to important information.

In reality, the dominant stakeholders of a large Western, namely Anglo-Saxon corporation are not shareholders, but rather high-ranking managers. Their dominance, often effectively uncontested, leads to a decision-making monopoly, while their responsibility for the outcome remains obscure. Among other things, they have obtained enormous power to set their own revenues at fantastically high levels, often without a linkage with the corporation's performance and profitability.

In this sense, Anglo-Saxon capitalism is not itself anymore. Some of its very basic concepts have ceased to apply.

Furthermore, this real Western corporate model is not in agreement with the basic idea of the market economy as such. It is a dictatorship, rent-seeking, and rent-taking based on personal power. Besides enormous economic losses it incurs, it destroys values and ideals embedded in the fabric of liberal Western societies, causing the deepest crisis of confidence since the late 1980s, when America was losing badly in its competition with rapidly rising Japan, and Eurosclerosis was the most popular definition for the status of major economies of the old continent.

Bankers' moves to aggressively protect their cosmic bonuses, even after their institutions collapsed and were bailed out by the state with the use of taxpayers' money, manifest a destruction of Western business and societal ethics, or rather their remnants. The financiers' most popular argument that unless the bonuses are left intact talented people (did they mean those talented people who had engineered the financial fiasco?) would not stay is both cynical and confusing. It goes against the basic principle the market economy rests upon: Businesspeople have to bear responsibility for their decisions and actions.

Logically, if this principle still really mattered, in such a situation it would have been irrelevant and ridiculous to pay *any* bonuses at all. Government bailouts should have been accompanied not only by bonuses bans, but also by mandatory replacements of all high-ranking managers of the business entities rescued, with punitive financial measures against those who were responsible for the failures. No government was bold enough to go that far.

The truth, and one of the greatest social injustices of the early twenty-first century, is that today, in the aftermath of the crisis, those who engineered it are mostly doing fine and living a jolly life, while millions of people it broke down are still struggling with its repercussions. This manifests one more failure of Western capitalism: a moral failure.

Or maybe, in the world of Western financial business the very notion of morality had already been killed altogether?

The investigation showed that in the wake of the crisis, in a desperate effort to arrange any cash flow, for example, the Wachovia

Bank, one of the largest in the United States (in 2008 it was acquired by Wells Fargo), laundered money of the Mexican drug mafia on a scale equaling one-third of Mexico's GDP. The Bank of America was also involved in operations of this kind (Winter 2010).

Surprisingly (or not surprisingly?) it did not become a big story in the news and was not widely discussed by the public. For Wachovia it was quite a happy end as it avoided criminal prosecution paying out almost a symbolic fine of $160 million. Meanwhile the bank reportedly had no way of checking $420 billion (?!) in transactions for possible money laundering activity (Anderson 2010). This is a bit too much, isn't it?

Chapter 11

Still, Western Capitalism Is Alive, But....

I n the wake of the crisis, the end of capitalism became a popular theme with Western politicians, economists, journalists, and the general public. As the governments were bailing out and nationalizing leading banks, insurance companies, and even some manufacturing firms, there was a lot of argument about the growing economic role of the state and the need to strengthen it in the longer term.

Calm Down: No End of Capitalism

However, this anticapitalist rhetoric had no sound conceptual basis and began to fade as soon as Western economies started recovering.

There is no medium- or long-term trend toward increasing state involvement in economic activities. The main pillars of the Western capitalist system: private companies as dominant players, market-based resource allocation, profit maximization as the major goal of company management, and market prices freely set by producers depending on supply and demand, remain intact.

Government Bailouts and Nationalizations Were a Temporary Step

Government bailouts and nationalizations were a temporary step, an emergency rescue operation. As targeted financial institutions and companies are restructured and put back on track, they are again sold out to private investors, and the state is even making profit on it. Government loans are also repaid.

Much of the $700 billion fund, established by the U.S. government to help ailing banks, AIG, GM, and Chrysler, was not actually disbursed. According to the Government Accountability Office, about $385 billion in cash had been handed out as of September 30, 2010, and almost $204 billion had been paid back. The fund made $28 billion on interest, dividends, and profit on investments. About $180 billion was outstanding.

The largest rescue package of $182 billion to save AIG is to be paid off by 2012. According to the estimates, at current levels, as of March 2011, the Treasury could make a profit up to $40 billion. AIG paid its $21 billion outstanding balance to the New York branch of the Federal Reserve in January 2011 (Gogoi 2011).

The U.S. government's last stake in Citigroup was sold in December 2010. Its share in GM (about one-third) is also being gradually transferred.

The rescue schemes, after all, turned out to be more of a commercial operation than a donation from state coffers. In this sense, the government deserves credit.

Yes, Western capitalism failed.

However, currently it is addressing its structural problems within its own systemic framework, learning lessons from the crisis. All the major parties involved—the state, financial institutions, and households—are trying to improve and act in a more reasonable way. They have no other choice.

Regulatory Framework Is Getting Better

The state is strengthening regulation and oversight of financial institutions, making steps to contain disruptive financial gambling. Transactions with structured products have been put under stricter control than before the crisis.

The Dodd-Frank Wall Street Reform and Consumer Protection Act passed by the U.S. Congress and signed into law by President Obama in July 2010, marked a significant, albeit belated, step forward toward establishing a regulation and risk-managing system capable of meeting challenges posed by a speedy innovation of financial products and risky speculative games with them. Among other things, the legislation puts an end to bailouts of financial institutions with taxpayers' money and establishes an advanced warning system on the stability of the economy.

The Act has endorsed the modified version of the P. Volcker Rule, limiting banks' investment in private equity funds and hedge funds as well as in trade for hedging purposes to no more than 3 percent of their Tier 1 capital. The banks' share also cannot exceed 3 percent of the ownership interest in the funds mentioned. (The rule articulated by P. Volcker, former Fed Chairman and the chair of the President's Economic Recovery Advisory Board, initially prohibited banks and institutions from owning or investing in equity funds and hedge funds altogether, as well as from engaging in any proprietary trading not on the behest of their clients. The aim was to restrain speculative investment.) The range of proprietary trading covered by the act turned out to be even wider than initially proposed by the administration.

The Act bans the so-called conflicts of interest: in other words, banks' dreadful financial gambling at the expense of their clients. It bars banks from creating financial instruments based on shaky assets, selling them to their clients, and then playing against those clients by betting on the instruments' failure. Banks have to disclose the full extent of their relations with hedge funds and equity funds to regulators and convince them that this relationship does not contain the conflicts of interest described.

Also, a range of nonbank financial institutions will be supervised by the Fed in the same way as if they were bank holding companies.

Before the Act was passed, investment advisers, having less than 15 clients during the previous 15 months and not holding themselves out to the general public as investment advisers, were exempt from the SEC registration requirement. This exemption has been eliminated, which means compulsory registration for many more investment advisers, hedge funds, and private equity funds.

Supervision of over-the-counter transactions with derivatives will also be strengthened. Besides, the Act encourages trading through exchanges and clearing houses of those derivatives that were traditionally traded over-the-counter.

The asset-backed securitization process has been improved by prohibiting hedging or transferring credit risk without retaining an interest with respect to the asset. Currently, for a residential mortgage, not less than 5 percent of the credit risk has to be retained.

Yet, there is still a lot to be done. For instance, at this point financial derivatives are not fully quantified on banks' financial statements (Gandel 2011).

Financial Institutions Recover and Improve Risk Management

Major Western banks and other financial institutions have started upon a recovery path, focusing on their core business and curtailing transactions with risky and potentially toxic instruments.

Banks' capital-to-asset ratios have increased, especially in the United States. As of the second half of 2011, the four major American banks (Bank of America, J.P. Morgan, Citigroup, and Wells Fargo) were holding capital equal to about 11 percent of their outstanding loans versus 9 percent at the end of 2008. The ratio for the average EU bank rose from 5.9 percent at the end of 2007 to 6.5 percent at the end of 2010 (Gandel 2010).

In 2010, the 10 largest European banks registered combined net profits equal to about $67 billion: 25 percent more than a year earlier (even though Germany and France imposed a special tax on banks' assets and liabilities). All of them were in the black except the Royal Bank of Scotland. The latter, however, also became profitable in the fourth quarter, and its annual net loss fell to one-third of the 2009 level.

Profits were generated first of all in the major area of business: commercial, especially retail, banking operations. UBS became profitable for the first time since 2006. BNP Paribas increased profits more than 30 percent, HSBC 2.2 times, and Société Générale more than fivefold (Nikkei 2011b).

However, as a legacy of the crisis, Europe has a tier of weak banks with thin capital reserves, significant outstanding investment in shaky assets, and unstable sources of financing. They are vulnerable to further shocks.

In the United States, in the fourth quarter of 2010, out of six major banks, only Bank of America suffered net losses as it was buying back nonperforming mortgage securities, while JPMorgan Chase, Wells Fargo, and Morgan Stanley enhanced their profits year-on-year 47 percent, 21 percent, and 88 percent respectively. The Citigroup registered net profits of $1.3 billion while a year ago it suffered a net loss. Goldman Sachs's net profits declined (Nikkei 2011c).

CDOs as a financial instrument are believed to have reached the point of no return. Investment banks working with structured products have come out with their customers' rescue plans, restructuring the products and extending their maturity.

Lenders are checking borrowers more thoroughly and tightening lending criteria: Today's major problem is not overlending, but rather a credit squeeze. Banks often refuse to lend even to quite reliable clients.

The monitoring of mortgage loan recipients has been significantly strengthened, containing the lending expansion—and posing problems of an entirely different character: sluggish demand for new homes and prolonged asset deflation.

The scale of the securitization of real estate loans in the United States has significantly declined and at the time of writing is mostly limited to the office and retail space segment less hit by the crisis than residential properties. In 2010, there were fewer than 10 securitizations of commercial real estate with a total value of no more than $10 billion, and market participants expect it to rise to $40–$55 billion in 2011, as opposed to $230 billion in 2007. They intend to act in a more prudent and reasonable way than they did in the precrisis period. "Nobody believes we will get back to 2007 numbers, because there were some lending practices that were not sustainable," says Ben Aitkenhead, head of U.S. CMBS (Commercial Mortgage-Based Securities) at Credit Suisse. "But reaching an annual figure of $100 billion within the next couple of years seems a realistic target" (Alexander 2011).

Also, notably, investors in CMBC such as managers of CDOs, off-balance-sheet structured investment vehicles (SIVs), and asset-backed commercial paper conduits (in other words, floating rate investors), have effectively disappeared. Today's buyers are more risk-averse fixed-rate investors: insurance companies, large fund managers, banks, and specialist hedge funds (Alexander 2011).

In postcrisis Europe, the amount and scale of securitization still remains negligible.

Overall, postcrisis Western financial capitalism is reassessing its mode of behavior, becoming more cautious and risk-conscious. In this new decade, it is starting to somewhat drift away from adventurous and destructive financial gambling. At least for the time being.

However, the legacy of the crisis is still there: The problems it posed are too big to be solved within a few years. Mortgage troubles remain a big impediment in the United States, significantly constraining business and revenues of major banks. As of autumn 2011, amid a continuing fall in housing prices, the number of borrowers seriously delinquent on their mortgage payments continues to increase. Also, banks are bearing big litigation losses due to lawsuits by both government and private investors over sour mortgage bonds (Gandel 2011).

In Europe, banks are facing new problems stemming from the sovereign debt crisis: Many government bonds they have purchased are becoming essentially a doubtful asset. Under this circumstance even the condition of the major players like Société Générale is causing a lot of concern.

Households Save More and Borrow Less

Finally, the crisis has made many Western households more financially conservative than they used to be. In some countries, there are signs of a slight rise in savings. Indebtedness is declining.

In the United States, the net household saving rate rose from 1.7 percent in 2007 to 4.3 percent in 2009 and then on to around 6 percent in late 2010—early 2011 (Bureau of Economic Analysis 2011a). The ratio of households' debt to disposable income in 2010 dropped to 118 percent from the record high of 130 percent registered in 2007 (Glick and Lansing 2010).

In 2009, the gross savings ratio of disposable income increased from a year earlier: from 1.5 percent to 7 percent in the United Kingdom, from 12.9 percent to 18.8 percent in Spain, from 6.4 percent to 8.8 percent in Portugal, and from 15.3 percent to 16.3 percent in France (Global Finance 2011).

In the United States and the United Kingdom, households' outstanding debt declined even in absolute terms, and the euro area registered a drastic fall of its growth rate.

The West has entered the adjustment stage needed to address structural problems that led to the crisis of 2008—2009. Western capitalism is becoming, or at least trying to become, more cautious, prudent, and reasonable. Though imposing constraints on growth in the short term, such adjustment, as long as it is persistent enough, will make America and Europe structurally stronger and in better shape to accelerate after it is over.

However, other structural impediments to growth are becoming more severe. The price for the unconventional stimulus policies of the crisis years is high, and the payment period will be long. Hard times have come.

Crocodile Attraction and Western Economies

In some game centers around Japan you can still find Crocodile Attraction—an exciting game that, I think, has a deep philosophical meaning. Its popularity peak has passed: High-tech computer games are on the offensive. Yet, I do hope that it will survive because it is unique, charming, and clever.

You insert a 100 yen coin into the machine and get a wooden hammer in your hand. With this hammer you have to strike the heads of around ten crocodiles emerging in turn from the holes on the backside and sliding straight toward the player along their lines: long thin hollows. If you strike a crocodile in its head before it reaches the final destination, it cries, "I am in pain," turns back, and disappears in the hole (to appear again in a few seconds). You are awarded grades. If you fail to get it before it reaches the final spot, it proudly makes a return trip leaving you at a loss. The trick is that crocodiles emerge from their holes at an increasingly high speed, some of them simultaneously, and at a certain point you don't have time and energy to strike them all—unless you work really hard.

Usually, you strike at one or two or maybe even three crocodiles, but at this very moment two or three new crocodiles appear and make their way forward uncaught.

This is exactly what has been happening to major Western economies since the beginning of the crisis of 2008–2009 until this current period. The West has managed to strike the heads of the crocodiles named "overlending and overborrowing," "low savings and unaffordable consumption," "poor monitoring, governance, and supervision," and "adventurous financial transactions." For the time being, they have been chased back inside their holes. However, while the Western governments and business communities were striking at their heads, other big crocodiles (in other words, big structural problems) were emerging anew and making their way ahead. And it appears to be very difficult if not impossible to send them back to their holes.

The West's biggest crocodiles of today are soaring public debts and a heavy welfare state burden. Marked by unprecedented government spending, the crisis of 2008–2009 made both problems much more acute than before.

Needless to say, China has a lot of crocodiles of its own. However, to continue the analogy, in the process of its rapid growth, it beats them one after another, continuing to run ahead at a high speed. On the contrary, to fight with its crocodiles, the West has to shift from one foot to another without any noticeable advance—just like a customer playing the game. The crocodiles don't let it move forward at a reasonably high speed. In other words, the West's structural problems exacerbated by the crisis are significantly slowing down its postcrisis growth pace and are likely to do so for quite a long period of time—perhaps for the whole decade or even longer.

Soaring Public Debts as the Biggest Crocodile

In 2008–2009, to keep the national economies afloat, Western governments were forced to compile stimulus packages on a scale never seen before—forgetting, for the time being, about budget constraints they were facing. It would be naïve to expect that such a spending extravaganza could go on without consequences in the longer term.

In the years prior to the crisis, most Western governments worked hard to curb budget deficits and achieved certain results (Table 11.1). However, huge spending during the crisis period largely devalued those efforts.

The change in the ratio of public gross debt to the GDP in a number of European countries (Italy, Greece, Spain, Sweden, as well as in the euro area as a whole) became V-shaped: Before the crisis it was declining, but in 2008–2009, surged again.

In France, the United Kingdom, Germany, and the United States, between 2000 and 2007 the ratio was already gradually increasing, but in 2008–2009 the pace of the increase accelerated dramatically.

Table 11.1 Public Gross Debt as Percent of the GDP

	2000	2007	2008	2009
Japan	135.4	167	173.8	192.9
Italy	121.6	112.4	114.7	128.8
Greece	114.9	104.3	104.6	119
Total OECD	69.6	73	79	90.3
Portugal	62	71.1	75.2	87
France	65.6	69.9	75.7	86.3
United States	54.5	61.9	70.4	83
UK	45.1	47.4	46.7	51.8
Germany	60.4	65.3	68.8	76.2
Spain	60.4	65.3	68.8	76.2
Sweden	64.3	47.4	46.7	51.8
Switzerland	52.4	46.5	42.4	41.6

SOURCE: OECD Economic Outlook 87 database, June 2010.

In Japan the situation was the worst of all: Though prior to 2007 the ratio was rising fast, in 2008–2009 the pace accelerated even further. Portugal's condition was similar, but the ratio itself much lower.

In the crisis years, outstanding public debt soared not only in the countries where heavy indebtedness had already become a major headache, such as Japan, Italy, or Greece, but also in the states where prior to the crisis the debt/GDP ratio had been comparatively low, such as the United States, the United Kingdom, France, Germany, and Portugal.

In Spain, Sweden and also the Netherlands, Finland, and Luxemburg, the debt burden remained a little less heavy, though it also noticeably increased (especially in Spain) in 2008–2009. Perhaps the only happy exception was Switzerland where the outstanding debt was declining all through the decade, including the crisis years.

For the OECD as a whole, the debt/GDP ratio was hovering around 70 percent in the 1990s, slightly increased by 2007, and rose to 90 percent in 2009. In the postcrisis period, almost all major Western states have no other choice but to fix a drastic reduction of the public debt as their priority task.

Currently the world's attention is focused on several European countries facing the deepest crisis of public finance and the sovereign bonds market: Greece (facing a default threat), Ireland, Portugal, and Spain, and also Italy, which have unveiled emergency austerity policies. However, the largest Western powers cannot escape debt reduction steps of an unprecedented scale as well.

In autumn of 2010, the British Conservative administration launched the largest public spending cuts in the country's postwar history: 81 billion pounds ($128 billion) of government spending has to be slashed by 2015. Along with some tax increases, they are expected to reduce the budget deficit by 109 billion pounds ($172 billion). Spending on health, education, and overseas aid will be maintained at current levels or increased, and government transport and carbon capture technology projects are to go as planned. However, all other spending has to be trimmed, with departments' expenditure cuts averaging 19 percent. About half a million public sector jobs will be lost (AP 2010).

In Germany, public spending is to be slashed by more than 80 billion euros ($96 billion) over the first four years of this decade. Up to 15,000 public sector jobs will be cut. A maximum structural deficit has to be reduced to just 0.35 of the GDP by 2016—a little more than one-tenth of the 3 percent level set by the EU stability and growth pact. Net spending cuts will gradually increase from 11.1 billion euros in 2011 to 16.1 billion euros in 2012, 25.7 billion euros in 2013, and 32.4 billion euros in 2014. New taxes will be imposed on the nuclear power industry and air travel, along with a bank levy (Peel 2010).

In France, the Sarkozy administration came out with a plan to reduce the central government's budget deficit from 152 billion euros ($207 billion) in 2010 to 92 billion euros in 2011. The overall public deficit (including the central government, local governments, and the welfare budget) is to be cut to 6 percent of the GDP in 2011 and to 2 percent in 2014—the largest budget correction of all the postwar period. More than 30,000 government employees will retire without replacement. State spending, other than the one to prop up the pension fund and to service the government debt, will be frozen at current levels, including transfers to local and regional governments. Closing of tax loopholes will mean a de facto tax increase for particular categories of workers and some insurance and property investment.

Europe is rapidly shifting toward financial conservatism. In the United States, while the Obama administration is in power, the situation remains more complicated.

President Obama is definitely not the right person to initiate and carry out large-scale budget spending cuts. He is basically comfortable with the state's active involvement in the economy, which, essentially, requires substantial funding. He favors raising taxes for the rich to support the poor. He is very keen about preserving and, where possible, strengthening social safety nets.

Even when, in the wake of the 2008–2009 spending spree, the situation with the U.S. public debt became critical, the President was not at all anxious to compile a financial austerity package. He showed much less persistence and political will to put the country's finances in order than the leader of any major European nation. Politically it was much easier for him to continue with big spending, underlining the intention to support a fragile recovery.

In the short term, this approach worked: In 2010 the U.S. economy appeared to be in better shape than that of any major European country—perhaps, with the exception of Germany. However, in the field of budget reforms, the administration lost time and gave the Republicans an excellent chance to fill the policy vacuum. Unfortunately for Obama, this is exactly the field that has come into the focus of public attention on the eve of the 2012 presidential election.

The president outlined his financial policy vision in a speech at George Washington University, only in April 2011. It was a package of tax increases and spending cuts aimed at reducing the deficit by $4 trillion by 2023. Tax hikes, first of all heavier taxation of the rich (through the abolition of the Bush tax cuts and closing of loopholes), were estimated to provide for one-fourth of the total reduction. Cuts were proposed in discretionary nondefense and defense spending, agricultural subsidies, federal pension insurance, and antifraud measures. Social safety nets were left basically untouched. Also, the President pledged to kick in the so-called debt fail-safe by 2014, which means the start of spending reduction across the board in case long-term deficit projections do not improve. Yet, in this case, too, it would not apply to Social Security, low-income programs, and medical benefits (Roth 2011).

For its part, the Republican-controlled House adopted, as a nonbinding blueprint, the austerity package of an entirely different character, announced by Paul Ryan, chairman of the House Budget Committee. The Ryan Plan calls for spending cuts of up to $5.8 trillion over 10 years—the greatest in American history; reduction of tax rates for corporations and wealthy families (but also elimination of tax loopholes), and significant cuts in social spending starting from the Medicaid program. Notably, right before the approval of the Plan, Congress adopted legislation cutting $38.5 billion out of the national budget for the remaining four and one-half months of the 2011 fiscal year, ending in September.

In September 2011 the President proposed a $3.1 trillion package of spending cuts and tax increases over 10 years from 2013. This time it included spending cuts on Medicare and Medicaid ($248 billion and $72 billion respectively) as well as cuts in farm subsidies and benefits for federal employees. One trillion dollars was to be saved by drawing down U.S. troops in Afghanistan and transferring to a civilian-led mission in Iraq. A $1.5 trillion tax increase would result from the expiration of tax cuts for the rich introduced under George W. Bush and elimination of tax loopholes for businesses. Tax increases were linked to job creation measures.

The neoconservative wave in the United States, not only in the political establishment, but also in American society in general (salute the Tea Party!), is gaining strength, and for President Obama it is becoming more and more difficult to go against the current, betting on the political capital he has gained during these several years. His room for maneuvering is becoming more and more limited.

Having won a comfortable majority in the House, the Republicans have started pressing the administration first and foremost on the financial policy issues, and it helped them to drastically change the domestic political scene within a surprisingly short period of time. As of early June of 2011, according to the opinion polls, the popularity rating of former Massachusetts Governor Mitt Romney, a GOP presidential candidate, has already caught up with that of the president.

In the economic and political context of the early 2010s, Obamanomics are doomed to fail. The president will either have to adopt a more proactive stance on spending cuts (rather than tax increases) and deficit reduction, or lose the election. America is also going neoconservative.

As never before, the West has to concentrate on putting its fiscal house in order. This is a tough reality of the early 2010s and the legacy of the crisis of 2008–2009. Things have gone too far. For instance, in France interest to be paid on the government debt is approaching the education budget—the biggest public expenditure item. The United States was technically on the verge of a default, until Congress finally raised the government's borrowing ceiling on the eve of the August 2, 2011, deadline. As a result, for the first time in history one of the major credit rating agencies, Standard & Poor's, lowered the Treasury Bonds' rating from AAA to AA+.

Even after the end of the crisis, Western economies remain sick. The pills needed to cure those sick men are so strong that, while taking them, they will be able to move along at only a slow pace, coughing and sniffing, if not bleeding.

For most Western governments, at least the first half of this decade will be a period of tough financial constraints, leaving very little room to use budget spending as a growth stimulant. Large-scale issuance of government bonds may crowd out private investment. It is also unfeasible to foster growth by easing monetary policy as interest rates are already extremely low, and inflationary pressures are on the rise. A mix of deep spending cuts and tax increases will negatively affect households' disposable income, curtail many economic activities, and cause social tensions if not unrest. Massive antigovernment demonstrations, sometimes violent, in the streets of Athens, Lisbon, Madrid, Paris, and so on may only be a prelude, and also a warning. Mass riots and looting in London and other British cities in August 2011 and, especially, Occupy Wall Street, are a tolling bell. These dramatic events first of all reflect despair and the wrath of the growing number of the have-nots feeling betrayed by their governments. More and more, they resemble the class warfare, almost in the Marxist sense.

To change the angle, financial austerity, logically, puts an end to a debate about the Western economies' shift toward state capitalism widely anticipated and often called for in the crisis years. Today governments simply cannot afford it.

Nevertheless, as mentioned, the West's economic future will largely depend on its ability, even under tough financial constraints, to do much more to help domestic businesses enhance their global competitiveness and capture markets in the developing world, especially China. America, Europe, and Japan need strong government policies supporting industrial upgrading and exports. If, amid a neoconservative drive, this dimension is forgotten, the global economic clout of major Western powers will be weakening at a growing speed.

The Welfare State Has to Be Trimmed More and Faster

Since the 1990s, as life expectancy was rising and birth rates and the share of the population in its working age falling, most Western, especially European countries started to overhaul their social security systems in order to contain the increase of taxes, social contributions, and social spending. As a result social security benefits, especially pensions and health insurance payments, have been gradually reduced in scale. A number of countries elevated the retirement age. To provide for the means of support in the postretirement years, in the case of disability and so on, people have to save more and more by themselves, entrusting the management of the money they have accumulated to pension funds and other financial institutions.

Still, in the 2000s, the ratio of public social expenditure to the GDP continued to rise in most Western countries—though with some notable exceptions like Germany and Sweden, which managed to bring it down (Table 11.2). Today's critical status of public finance makes it necessary to do everything possible to reverse or at least stop the trend.

The West has to return to the roots of the social security concept. Basically, public social security payments are supposed to provide a *minimal basic* living standard, and not a cozy free lunch. For instance, high replacement rates (the ratio of public pension payments to the income from work the beneficiary received before retirement) in a number of countries, especially those facing grave public finance problems (for instance, in Greece it has reached around 90 percent), can hardly be sustained.

A big welfare state may badly undermine work motivation—an old problem coming to the forefront again in the wake of the growing global competition, especially from China.

Table 11.2 Gross Public Social Expenditure as Percent of GDP (%)

	2001	2007
France	32.0	32.8
Sweden	33.6	32.1
Italy	27.1	28.8
Germany	29.8	28.4
Finland	27.4	28.2
Spain	22.3	24.1
UK	22.1	23.3
Japan	18.9	20.3
US	16.3	17.4
OECD total★	22.3	28.0

★OECD-23 for 2001 and OECD-27 for 2007.
SOURCE: OECD. Social Expenditure Database.

While people out of work count on high social security benefits comparable to their earnings in times when they had a job, those who have a job are not motivated to work harder, as a substantial part of the increase of their earnings will be eaten out by high taxes and public social security contributions. On their part, employers restrain new hiring because they have to share the heavy social security burden. It pushes up unemployment rates.

Overall, too big a welfare state reduces the efficiency of the use of human resources—the fundamental issue of primary importance the West has to address in a really serious way, not least in the wake of the Chinese challenge.

Besides, one more somewhat tricky welfare state–related problem exists, deserving close attention. It is still largely unspoken because of its sensitivity. The creation and expansion of public social security systems were driven by the quest for social justice. However, today those systems have turned out to be very unfair toward working families, especially those in their 30s and 40s—the age when, logically, consumption activities should reach their peak. Those families have to pay more and more to support the elderly and other social security beneficiaries, while at this life stage their own living expenses, especially buying a home and bringing up children, usually reach their peak, and while in today's developed societies a substantial portion of the elderly and other people they have to support are richer than themselves.

The picture is one of a pale-faced worn-out guy in his 30s or 40s, always on the run and, due to a tight family budget, thinking twice before buying an extra can of beer at a grocery store or a cup of coffee at Starbucks, having to support well-to-do guys in their 60s, 70s, and beyond who are relaxing a lot, having a jolly time playing cricket or golf, traveling around the world for their own pleasure, and maybe even buying, without any hesitation, diamonds and furs for their wives and Cartier watches for themselves. Mind you, the former guy can hardly expect to be provided the same amount of benefits from public social security funds when he himself hits 65 or 70.

Of course, this sketch is grotesque and it does not pretend to grasp the whole picture. A lot of elderly people are not so well-to-do and need genuine social protection provided by the state. However, it represents a very important dimension of the problem. As the economy and society develop and mature, more and more people become financially capable of providing their living after retirement (either all the living expenses or their substantial part), their medical expenses, and so on by themselves, without relying on income redistribution by the state. And they should do it. High dependency on public social security has to be limited to those who really cannot do without relying on state protection.

Currently, Western powers have no choice but to trim the welfare state on a larger scale and at a higher speed than they did before the crisis. Within the five years prior to 2015, the United Kingdom will ax about 18 billion pounds ($28.5 billion) from welfare payments, raise the pension age to 66 by 2020, or four years earlier than initially planned (it will alter retirement plans for about 5 million people and save 5 billion pounds annually), and deprive better-off families from child benefit payments. Lower-income families will be restricted to a dozen social benefits including those related to housing payments (AP 2010).

Germany currently stops short of pension cuts, but is moving to reduce social security and unemployment benefits—not the least in order to amplify incentives for unemployed people to find work and not to depend on generous state support. There will be more means-testing of benefits for the unemployed. Child allowances for unemployed parents will be cut. Overall, within four years from 2011, social spending is to be cut by 5 billion euros (Peel 2010).

In the United States, the Obama administration finds it increasingly difficult to keep social safety nets intact, and the Republican-backed Ryan Plan calls for cutting Medicaid (the medical insurance scheme for the poor and disabled) and transforming it into a grant program run by the states. Medicare is to evolve into a system under which the government provides future retirees (people who are currently under 55) with vouchers—in other words, subsidies—to buy private insurance plans. However, the vouchers are likely to gradually lose their value, as they will not catch up with the rising medical costs.

In the 1930s, Western societies started to create the welfare state. In the post-war decades they significantly increased its scale. At the end of the twentieth century, they began to curtail it. The crisis of 2008–2009 left them with no alternative but to speed up this process.

It has to be done; otherwise, Western societies will become financially unsustainable and economically powerless.

However, out of all kinds of state spending cuts, trimming of public social security systems is the most painful, politically difficult, and socially explosive exercise. Not surprisingly, it is already meeting enormous resistance, especially on the European continent. It is a bitter fight, causing social strains and unrest, which may significantly impede growth and destabilize Western economies.

Also, last but not least, trimming the welfare state makes people feel socially insecure, undermining confidence in their own future. The mentality of an average Western household is more and more entering the tomorrow-it-will-be-worse-than-today territory, inducing it to tighten the belts. (In China it is the reverse.) This phenomenon influences the West's economic strength in the negative.

Chapter 12

Is China Structurally Stronger Than the West?

igh households' indebtedness, low savings, uncontrolled
expansion of credit to marginal borrowers, adventurous
games with structured financial products and poor risk
management, public debts hitting critical highs, and the urgent need to
accelerate the trimming of the welfare state—this is the list of key
structural problems that either drove Western economies into the crisis
or are exacerbating it in its aftermath.

By contrast, today's Chinese economy is mostly free of and largely
immune to all those structural diseases. Also, it is in a good position to
prevent their outburst in the future.

A lot has been said and written about China's structural weaknesses. The time has come to assess its structural strengths. It may seem
improbable, but compared to the West, the economy of today's China
appears to be structurally stronger and healthier. This is one of the
major reasons the global power balance is shifting in its favor.

Improvement of Lending Practices and Persistent Fight with Overheating

As mentioned, Chinese households' indebtedness is meager while their saving rates are remarkably high. There is the Western culture of living on debt, and there is the Chinese culture of minimizing family debts and keeping them under tight control. Thus, in China there is effectively no room for unaffordable consumption prompted by excessive household borrowing.

In the corporate sector, Chinese banks, most of all state-owned banks as major lenders, are extending massive loans to domestic companies. Usually two major problems are raised in this regard. First, there are concerns that a substantial portion of loans—especially those extended to state-owned enterprises—may be politically motivated and lack commercial rationale. Second, there is lot of anxiety about the fact that the government and the central bank often fail to keep credit expansion within the limits they set, which allegedly exacerbates the threat of overheating and creates an asset bubble.

Such concerns, however, are usually exaggerated.

Indeed, politically motivated loans to particular Chinese companies, especially state-owned, are still extended, and some poorly performing enterprises may get funding to keep afloat. However, the major trend is the reverse. Since the start of market reforms, China has been making a really big shift from soft to hard budget constraints for enterprises. As times goes by, generally it is becoming more and more difficult for companies, state-owned enterprises (SOEs) included, to get funding from the state, and the proportion of the fund-raising done by themselves in accordance with the market rules is steadily increasing.

Already in the 1980s, the government effectively terminated the SOEs' direct budgetary financing. Yet, until the launch of the SOE reform in the second half of the 1990s, state banks had to continuously provide massive loans under the government's directives without the right to squeeze or terminate commercially unviable credit. With the start of the reform, however, this practice significantly decreased in scale.

Back in 2003, the state recapitalized the four major banks and after that embarked on their corporatization. The latter was marked by consecutive world records in terms of the amount of funds they raised through the IPO, reflecting high expectations of the investment community.

The Chinese leadership understands too well that commercially unviable financing and lending are a potential bomb whose explosion can undermine the very foundation of the economic system it is creating—and also the foundation its own power is resting on. The collapse of the Soviet Union and other conventional socialist economies provided crucially important empirical evidence in this regard. Hence, it is doing its best to make more, not less, state lending commercially viable. Even the three so-called policy banks (China Development Bank, Export-Import Bank, and Agricultural Development Bank of China) are increasingly relying on self-initiated commercial loans, while the proportion of subsidized government-directed lending is falling (KPMG 2010).

As for excessive bank lending, which sometimes exceeds government-imposed limits, it is important to examine the problem within the context of China's macroeconomic policy as a whole.

For three decades the key feature of this policy has been a persistent stance to neutralize the overheating threat. The architects of China's macroeconomic policy are always on the alert. The record clearly shows that the government and the central bank recognize this threat very well and, when necessary, do not hesitate to tighten monetary policy in a very resolute manner.

In the late 1990s, China's monetary policy was expansionary in 1998–2002 when the deflationary trend was a major concern. It was tightened already in 2003 and grew increasingly restrictive up to the global downturn years. It was loosened in 2008–2009, but tightened again in 2010, only several months after the start of the global recovery.

To prevent overheating and contain the financial bubble, the Chinese government utilizes a wider range of monetary policy tools than its Western counterparts. For example, along with setting lending limits and increasing mandatory bank reserves to be held in the People's Bank of China, it designates industries with excess production capacity where new investment projects are put under direct state supervision, or intervenes into the real estate market, restricting purchases and reselling of high-end property, which is likely to become a target for speculators.

Furthermore, when inflation risks are considered high, it does not stop short of directly guiding sellers not to raise prices for important consumer and production goods.

Overall, at this point China has a very impressive record (perhaps, more impressive than that of any other big country) of avoiding, or rather preventing overheating and the asset bubble threat. Seen from this angle, inability to keep credit within imposed limits appears to be just a technical problem emerging in the process of the implementation of a policy that basically works.

Enhancing Regulatory Standards for Banks

It would be safe to say that overall China has been fighting excessive lending and financial bubbles more persistently and successfully than most countries in the West.

In the wake of the Western financial crisis, the China Banking Regulatory Commission (CBRC) has made further steps to raise regulatory standards through increased capital requirements, loan ratios, and impairment rules. In the cities that have experienced excessive growth of property prices, it has initiated stress testing on banks to assess the impact of the worst-case scenario of a 50 to 60 percent price fall. Previous tests assumed drops of up to 30 percent. (The latter would have led to an estimated 2.2 percent rise of real estate nonperforming loans.) Banks have also been instructed to conduct stress tests for loans to industries facing overcapacity problems like cement, steel, and construction materials (KPMG 2010).

The condition of Chinese banks' loans portfolio is improving and currently, at least, does not cause serious concerns. According to KPMG, out of 153 banks it surveyed in 2009, three had NPL ratios above 5 percent, 21 between 2 percent and 5 percent, 115 below 2 percent, and 14 did not provide NPL data (KPMG 2010). According to the CBRC, as of the end of 2010, nonperforming real estate loans by Chinese commercial banks amounted to 44.0 billion yuan, or no more than 1.26 percent of all outstanding loans (Nikkei 2011d).

Next, Chinese financial institutions don't play with tricky structured financial instruments the way their Western counterparts do—both because of tight government regulations and the lack of market infra-structure as well as financiers who are versed in such transactions.

It goes without saying that financial sectors in China and in the West are going through different development stages. However, in the global economic arena China and the West are competing in a real-time format—and in this competition, paradoxically, China's earlier stage works as a source of strength, shielding it from financial gambling risks the West is fighting, often unsuccessfully. Also, there is little doubt that from now on, while further developing its financial sector, gradually liberalizing it and introducing new financial instru-ments, China will act much more cautiously than most of its Western counterparts, paying much more attention to accommodating and minimizing associated risks.

At present Chinese banks are actively diversifying their areas of business and widening the range of financial services. Non-interest incomes are becoming increasingly important. They are entering such areas as leasing, insurance, private banking, and trust. Authorities are steadily proceeding with deregulation. For instance, in 2009–2010 listed banks were allowed to trade bonds on the stock exchanges, and a pilot program was launched for establishing consumer finance compa-nies in Beijing, Tianjin, Shanghai, and Chengdu. Many banks are set-ting up or acquiring new financial services platforms.

However, at the same time, the CBRC is adopting a tough stance regarding the management of additional risks posed by such diversi-fication. Among other things, it requires banks to spinoff subsid-iaries they set in other sectors in case the latter's returns on assets or equity are below the average for their sector for a prolonged period. Supervision of new wealth management products is also strength-ened in order to protect consumers' interests. When offering personal wealth management, commercial banks are required to be prudent, to provide full information disclosure, and to properly manage risks, refraining from structuring wealth funds in financial products with high risks or with overly complicated structures (KPMG 2010).

In the West it is often argued that a wide variety of financial instruments, including risky ones, is needed to create money, which is invested in various industries. Today Chinese financial institutions are not working with many risky and tricky financial instruments popular in the West. Nevertheless, they provide plenty of funds for the country's industries—sometimes, according to Chinese financial authorities, even more than necessary. Today it is Western businesses that are facing a tighter credit squeeze.

Healthy Public Finance

Contrary to the West, China's public finance is preserved in a very healthy condition. At the beginning of the 2000s, the national government's (includes the central and local governments) budget deficit equaled 2.2 to 2.6 percent of the GDP. In 2004–2006, the ratio fell to 1.1 to 1.3 percent. In 2007, the budget was in surplus, and in 2008 the deficit reached just 0.4 percent of the GDP (author's calculations based on National Bureau of Statistics 2010).

Not surprisingly, for China the 4 trillion yuan stimulus package did not pose a major budget problem, and at the beginning of the 2010s the government still has a lot of room to use budget funds to facilitate economic growth, boost strategically important industries, promote R&D, and so on.

Also, China is noticeably increasing social spending. Its expenditure on social security and welfare increased from 3.9 percent of the GDP in 2000 to 5.3 percent in 2007.

Yet, the scale remains incomparable with that in any Western country. It is 10 percentage points less than the OECD average (Kujis 2008). A low level of social protection for those who need it most (especially for rural citizens), in combination with exacerbating employment problems and growing income disparities creates substantial social frictions. However, any social unrest, even at an embryonic form, is suppressed by the Communist regime with an iron fist.

At the same time, the Communist Party and the government have put the development and expansion of the social security network on the top of their domestic policy agenda. There is a solid financial basis to raise social expenditure further, making more and more people feel that tomorrow will be better than today. Social spending increases work as a socially stabilizing factor—by making people more confident in their tomorrow, they induce them to gradually reduce savings and increase consumption. In contrast, in the West spending cuts cause social tensions, if not disturbances, undermining people's confidence in their future.

In this decade the growth of China's social spending will accelerate—not least because its population is rapidly aging. The financial burden of working families will grow—especially as the population of the working age is likely to peak out around 2015. Nevertheless, China will surely avoid the Western trap of excessive (and unsustainable) social spending, resulting in a too heavy social security contributions burden. It is in a good position to create a financially sound and sustainable social security system, sticking to a healthy principle of providing just minimal basic living standards worthy of a human being at the present stage of the country's economic development.

Overall, the answer to the question posed in the title of this chapter is apparently positive. Yes, the difference in economic development stages aside, today the Chinese economy appears to be structurally stronger than major economies of the West. Structural strength, coupled with good macroeconomic condition, works as one of the major driving forces of change in the global power balance.

This brings us to the next issue of major importance: the essence of the Chinese model of capitalism and of its evolution.

Chapter 13

The Chinese Model
of Capitalism

Perhaps the most popular definition of the economic system of today's China is state capitalism as opposed to the Western-style liberal market economy with private companies at its core. It can hardly be denied that, at this point, compared to the West, in the Chinese economy there is more state, and, compared to China, in the Western economies there is more private entrepreneurship. Still, this conceptual framework is too simplistic—first of all because it underestimates the role of change.

The Need for a New Conceptual Framework

While retaining differences from Western economic systems, especially regarding the role of the state, China is accommodating more and more elements of conventional Western capitalism, first of all

Anglo-Saxon capitalism as the latter's classical model. This process of accommodation and the ability to accommodate are the sources of China's economic strength. Remaining different, it is becoming more and more similar to the West in many important respects. China's economic system appears to be a mix created by this dialectical game of similarities and differences.

The increase of its economic power is supported both by market incentives, which are becoming stronger and stronger (in some respects significantly stronger than in the West), and by large-scale government intervention. It is crucially important that, when intervening in the economy, the government remains promarket enough, or pragmatic enough, not to undermine market incentives.

Basically, the emergence of China as a new economic giant underlines the fact that the economic system of a nation influences its growth and power first of all not through its static condition (the way it looks at this particular moment), but through the dynamics of its evolution and adaptation to the changing internal and external environment.

The economies of the West are losing their market-driven dynamism. In contrast, the Chinese economy is growing and increasing its strength exactly on the energy of its promarket drive.

Within the three decades of reforms, in terms of its systemic transformation, China achieved three results of a historical importance.

The Chinese System Is Not State Capitalism: A Great Shift to Private Property

First, it made a large-scale shift from state to private property.

Between 1996 and 2003, the number of state-owned enterprises (SOEs) fell from 114,000 to 34,000, and half of the decline occurred due to privatization (Knowledge & Wharton 2006). Have a look at Table 13.1 to see what happened after that. The shift is continuing on a large scale. Between 2003 and 2008, the share of state-owned and state holding companies (the latter may also have private and other investors, but the state owns the majority stake) in the total number of industrial enterprises decreased from 22.7 percent to 5.0 percent, and their share in the total industrial output from 40.8 percent to 28.4 percent. Their

Table 13.1 The Number of Industrial Enterprises and Gross Industrial Output by Type of Enterprise

	2002		2008	
	Number of Enterprises	Gross Output (100 million yuan)	Number of Enterprises	Gross Output (100 million yuan)
Total	181,557	110,776	426,113	507,448
	100.0%	100.0%	100.0%	100.0%
State-owned	41,125	45,179	21,313	143,950
and state-holding	22.7%	40.8%	5.0%	28.4%
Private	49,176	12,951	136,340	245,850
	27.1%	11.7%	32.0%	48.5%
Limited Liability	22,846	20,070	62,835	108,571
	12.6%	18.1%	14.8%	21.4%
Shareholding	5,998	14,119	9,422	50,204
	3.3%	12.8%	2.2%	9.9%
With funds from	19,546	13,669	35,578	51,308
Hong Kong,	10.8%	12.3%	8.4%	10.1%
Macao, and Taiwan				
Foreign-funded	14,920	18,790	42,269	98,486
	8.2%	17.0%	9.9%	19.4%
Collective-owned	23,477	9,619	11,737	8,956
	12.9%	8.7%	2.8%	1.8%
Cooperative	10,193	3,202	5,612	3,829
	5.6%	2.9%	1.3%	0.8%

SOURCE: China Statistical Yearbook.

absolute number fell by half. On the contrary, the share of private companies increased from 27.1 to 32.0 percent and from 11.7 percent to 48.5 percent respectively. Their absolute number almost tripled.

The shares of limited-liability enterprises and foreign-funded companies are rising (the former, however, include entirely or partially state-funded companies), while the shares of enterprises of traditional types, usually closely controlled by the state—collectives and cooperatives—are declining.

As far as the ownership structure is concerned, China's economic system is not state capitalism as an antipode of the Western-style liberal market economy. It is a constantly *evolving* mixture of state-owned companies, private firms of various types, and the third sector. As such evolution gains strength, the share of the private sector is steadily rising, and so is its influence on the economy and society. In an important step, manifesting this change, at the beginning of this decade, private business-people were allowed to join the Communist Party.

Creating Market-Style State-Owned Companies

Second, state-owned companies have been put into a competitive environment where they have to rely more and more on themselves and less on the state, and to work hard to become profitable.

Though they remain the core part of the Chinese economy, their status is drastically changing. The conventional perception of an SOE is that of an enterprise operating under tight supervision of a government agency and relying on the state coffers for funding, shielded from competition, and pursuing the goals of the government's economic and social policy (such as achieving certain numerical targets for production of particular goods, providing employment, or even supporting social welfare institutions like hospitals or kindergartens). These goals are often achieved at the expense of commercial viability and profitability. Therefore the government has to provide financing to keep the enterprise going.

This perception has to be reconsidered. A different, nonconventional type of SOE also exists and, furthermore, plays an increasingly important role in many emerging market countries in Asia and beyond; that is to say, SOE-market-style. Run by professional managers with a high degree of decision-making authority, they do not rely on the state's soft financing but borrow at commercial rates or raise funds at the capital market. They fully participate in competition both domestically and, more and more often, internationally. They pursue profit maximization as a major goal. In such companies, private investors often hold a minority stake. They may be listed on the stock exchanges at home and overseas.

The SOEs of this kind are often more efficient, competitive, and dynamic than private companies.

The SOEs' shift from the traditional to the market-style pattern is a major source of China's structural transformation, giving its economy enormous energy to grow.

This is the direction of change, its major vector. In real life, many Chinese state-owned companies are currently still on their way between the two patterns described.

Since the start of the market reforms, step-by-step, the government has been reducing the scope of SOEs' products covered by the direct planning system, which kept the state responsible for financing, supply of necessary equipment and intermediate goods, price setting, and selling the products. The so-called *zhenqqi fenkai* policy was launched, meaning the separation of the government's functions from enterprises' business operations. More and more, SOEs were operating within the market framework, making their own decisions about the contents and volumes of production, prices, transaction partners, and so on. The state has been imposing on them increasingly hard financial constraints: Direct budget financing was effectively terminated in the 1980s. As time goes by, it is increasingly difficult for them to rely on government subsidies or soft loans and, especially, to be bailed out when they are poorly managed. (The increase of state financing and softening of its conditions in 2008–2009 was a short-term phenomenon—an emergency step in the wake of the dramatic worsening of global economic conditions.) According to official statistics, as many as 3,658 state companies failed between 1994 and 2005 (McKinsey 2007).

At the first stage of the large SOE reform launched in 1997, the state-owned companies were transformed into corporations, and part of their stock was sold to private investors. Some of them were listed. The second stage began in the middle of the 2000s. Emphasis was put on their reorganization, refocusing, self-reliance, and competitiveness.

In December, 2006, the State Assets Management Commission announced the program of the SOE structural adjustment, consisting of three major pillars: concentration in the sectors important for national security and in the basic industries like infrastructure and energy; government-initiated bankruptcy procedures for poorly performing companies with no prospects of improvement; and the reduction of the number of large SOEs owned by the central government from the initial 159 to 80–100 by 2010 through mergers, acquisitions, and other measures (Institute of Chinese Affairs 2006).

China's strategy is to create a limited number of strong and well-managed large SOEs, making at least part of them highly competitive global players.

In this regard, it is time to reconsider the concept of government as an enterprise owner. In a market-style SOE, it often behaves (as it has no viable alternative) not as a bureaucratic machine pursuing its own power and not as a promoter of some supreme political interests, but as a demanding majority stakeholder pressing managers to maximize profitability and investors' returns.

In a very important development, Chinese state-owned companies are starting to establish systems of corporate governance, learning from and largely replicating the Western experience, but also reflecting national specifics: first of all, the need to find a place for the Communist Party as an owner of and a stakeholder in an eventually *capitalist enterprise*.

Says John Thornton, the ex-president of Goldman-Sachs and one of the few Westerners serving on the boards of several major Chinese companies, including state-owned telecom giant China Network Communications (China Netcom) where he initiated the establishment of the corporate governance committee, and the Industrial and Commercial Bank of China:

> The reality is this: The Chinese want to adopt state-of-the-art corporate governance practices that pass Western tests. On the other hand, . . . they also want to build a system that works for China. . . . In Netcom we defined specific roles for the Communist Party and left the rest to the board. The Party participates and votes on key matters through nominated directors on the board, but fewer than half of the board members are party designees. We clearly defined the boundaries for party mandates for senior executive appointments, company strategy development and key investments. We gave authority to nominate CEO and CFO candidates back to the board. The CEO now owns the strategy-setting process and is supported by a newly created strategy department. We also set up formal channels to communicate better with Netcom's shareholders. . . . We defined the roles and duties of the board committees and secretariat, including

responsibilities for managing risks. . . . The nominating committee consists of five directors, three of whom are party designees and two who are external. In this way the party, as a majority shareholder, is able to veto candidates in committees, but external directors are able to provide significant input to all directors before the board discusses any candidacy. (McKinsey 2007)

It is the start of a step-by-step corporate revolution. The key point is the creation of a system making it possible to govern a state-owned corporation, in this case Netcom, as a business organization with a proper set of checks and balances in the way similar to a private company. The chairman of Netcom never stops saying that there is no contradiction between party influence (in other words, between the state's interest) and the protection of minority shareholders because their goals are the same: Netcom's success in business (McKinsey 2007). This is the essence of the new philosophy of the state's involvement whose goal is to facilitate, in the capacity of owner, the emergence and development of highly efficient and competitive business entities.

To pursue this goal, the state has to open them up to private investors, both domestic and foreign. The door is opening wider and wider, though gradually. A stratum of private investors actively buying state-owned companies' stock is emerging—both institutional and individual. Not surprisingly, many of them are related to China's ruling elite.

The stock market reform, launched in 2005, made it possible to trade previously untradeable SOEs' shares owned by the government, which comprised about two-thirds of the total value of stocks listed on the Shanghai and Shenzhen Exchanges. The following year almost all listed companies, in which the state owned stock, put their previously nontradable shares on sale, which led to a dramatic rise of their capitalization and enhanced the role of private investors.

Unloading of nontradable shares paved the way for the market-driven reshuffle of the corporate structure through mergers and acquisitions not initiated or controlled by the state. Some leading companies—China's number one and the world's number five steel producer Baosteel is a representative example—have launched aggressive acquisitions strategies.

In the mid-2000s, the government lifted the ban on the transfer of the shares owned by the state and SOE to foreign investors.

With the introduction in December 2002 of the qualified foreign institutional investor scheme, overseas investors approved by China Securities Regulatory Commission—fund managing, insurance, security companies, and commercial banks—were allowed to buy yuan-quoted A-shares initially available only for domestic investors. A single investor can acquire up to a 10 percent stake in a single company, and a combined share of up to 20 percent for all eligible investors is permitted (Tselichtchev & Debroux 2009).

Fierce Competition and the Culture of Self-Responsibility

Third, as a result of the market reforms, China has created an economy and society characterized by a very high degree of competition. It refers not only to growing competition among companies (including the one among companies with different forms of ownership), but also to a very competitive and flexible labor market stimulating motivation and individual effort and reinforcing the culture of self-responsibility. In many respects in today's China there is more competition than in America and Europe.

For example, according to the latest survey of 246 business executives from 33 countries working in China for an average of 7.4 years, conducted by China-Europe International Business School (CEIBS), 42.44 percent of the executives said that competition in China was tougher than in their country of origin, and 26.05 percent replied that it was much tougher (Fernandez, J Fenster, and Loane 2011).

China's incomparably lower level of state social spending results not only in a better state of public finance, but also in a much stronger link between people's incomes and their work effort, skills, and productivity. In this regard, labor motivation there is significantly higher. Today it is the Chinese, not the Western society, who are providing stronger incentives for an individual to take his life into his own hands. In this respect China is more capitalist, or more Western (if we assume that the West gave birth to a conventional capitalist system) than the West.

Making people work under stronger market pressures, China is also demonstrating higher ability to accommodate them: in other words, to make its citizens accept and tolerate those pressures without social turmoil.

Chinese society has a much higher degree of tolerance for the pains the market economy is causing: income disparities, low pay for a large number of workers, cuts of the excessive labor force by companies, unemployment, and underemployment. When signs of social unrest appear, it is suppressed by the regime. The Communist Party is enforcing capitalism.

There is a lot of talk about China's increasing income disparities as one of its major social problems and challenges. No doubt, it is a problem. However, let us not forget that expanding income gaps—or shall we say income differentiation?—stem from a low degree of the state's involvement in the labor market and a small scale of income redistribution through social transfers. In this regard, they stimulate labor effort, providing a very strong incentive for the capable and talented—and this provides a strong impetus for economic growth.

There are two patterns of the increase of income gaps. The first one, both socially explosive and economically detrimental, is the rise of absolute incomes of high-income families on the one hand and the fall of those of low-income families on the other. The rich become richer, and the poor poorer.

The second pattern is fundamentally different: Absolute incomes of both high-income and low-income households are rising, but the former's rise is faster. Of course, it makes people, especially those belonging to the low-income group, frustrated with increasing income inequality, which is often perceived as social injustice. It may cause social tensions. However, at the same time this pattern provides a very strong stimulus for economic growth: first, because it encourages the work effort, as the prospect of a higher income and better life is there for the households of all income groups; and second, because low-income families are also improving their living standards and becoming increasingly active consumers.

China is a typical example of pattern number two.

Chinese Capitalism: Definition

The economic system of today's China is *state-private capitalism* based on a mixture of forms of ownership, with private businesses playing an increasingly important role. It is incorporating more and more elements of conventional Western capitalism. It is generating increasingly strong market incentives for companies of all forms of ownership and provides a highly competitive environment. At the same time, unbound by any constraints stemming from the ideology of the free market, the Chinese state actively—much more actively than in any Western country—intervenes in the economy in order to support industries and companies on the one hand, and to contain the threats of excessive lending, high-risk financial transactions, and asset bubbles on the other. By and large, such intervention does not inhibit market mechanisms.

This model of capitalism has contributed a lot to China's emergence as a new economic superpower.

It showed a remarkable structural strength and problem-solving ability all through the decades of market reforms. Just think. In the 1980s–2000s, China was the only major economy in the world that did not experience a negative annual growth or even a slowdown in any way resembling a slump. It was the only major country that managed to prevent painful bursts of asset bubbles. Slowly but surely, gradually but steadily, it has been tackling its major social and economic problems: starting from the agricultural reform and overcoming food shortages, and then on to developing various kinds of nonstate enterprises and increasing the supply of basic consumer goods; opening up the economy for foreign investors and liberalizing imports; creating self-reliant SOEs and making them operate in the competitive environment; recapitalizing banks and resolving the nonperforming loans issue; strengthening social safety nets; promoting the development of inland provinces; and so on. Currently, in the same evolutionary but persistent way, it is addressing such key problems as stability of energy and natural resources supplies, energy efficiency, and environment protection.

A Digression about China's Structural Weaknesses and Political Evolution

China has a lot of structural problems. Almost all of them are similar to those faced by other developing nations that are at a similar stage of economic development. However, they are often more acute and visible to the whole world because of China's unique size. Their list is well known. A significant portion of manufacturers are inefficient, low-tech, and polluting enterprises. There is high latent unemployment and underemployment in the rural areas. Large-scale migration to the cities overstrains their infrastructure causing a lot of ultra-urbanization pains. Obvious mismatch exists between the labor supply (unskilled and low-skilled laborers prevail) and demand (more skilled laborers capable of handling industrial upgrading are needed). And so on, and so forth. . . .

Discussions of China's present and future usually focus on a gentlemanly set of problems. They are often looked upon as critical and posing a threat of an abrupt and disruptive economic downturn, social and political turmoil or, in the extreme case, the country's collapse. Such views do not look convincing. The gentlemanly set of problems is manageable, especially for China with its remarkable ability to address crucial issues through a *gradual, evolutionary, but persistent change.*

Let us have a look at a conventional Problems List.

Aging Population and Labor Shortages?

Yes, population of the working age is apparently approaching its peak and will start to decline in the second half of this decade.

However, labor force constraints can and most likely will be off-set by further gains in labor productivity. Also, there is still a lot of underused human resources in the countryside (about 40 percent of all Chinese laborers live in rural areas) whose migration to the cities will continue to boost labor supply.

As for the growing number and share of elderly people, China with its high growth rates, healthy public finance, currently very small social spending, and the absence of high expectations toward social safety nets in the future, is in a good position to address the population aging issue in a realistic and financially sustainable way. The West, not China, will have more difficult problems to fix in this area.

Growing Income Gaps?

Well, indeed, they are growing, but, on the other hand, low-income families are mostly elevating their earnings and consumption standards; social safety nets are improving; and, overall, today's China provides a lot of opportunities to enhance revenues and live a better life to those who really want to make it.

Intra-Regional Development Gaps Threatening the Country's Integrity?

Not at all. It is not a critical problem as less developed provinces are becoming the country's major growth engines and the state has enough financial and other resources to support and amplify the trend.

Environmental Damage Endangering the Very Basis of Human Life?

No doubt, a whole lot of issues have become critical. However, China is more and more establishing the position of one of the world leaders in most areas of green business (see Part Three), starting to tackle the environmental problems in the same *gradual, evolutionary, but persistent* manner it tackled the other ones.

And, finally, is there **a threat of a big political and social turmoil that may occur as people's anger with the authoritarian Communist regime and undemocratic political system bursts out and they take to the streets?**

Chinese people's dissatisfaction with the regime is really strong and apparently growing, impacted by numerous cases of power abuse, rampant corruption, and tough restrictions on the freedom of speech and other violations of basic human rights.

A fresh memory of mine. . . . Some three or four years ago, during a reception in honor of a group of Chinese professors visiting Japan, two of them approached me for a greeting and asked a tough question: "Sensei, why don't you write plainly that China's present political system is outdated and has to be changed? It worked, but now it has ceased to work. For us it is kind of problematic to write such a thing. Why don't you?"

What could I say to this?

For sure, democracy and human rights have a basic, universal value and are perhaps not less (or even more?) important than economic growth and rising living standards. In this sense, yes, offenses of human rights; brutal crackdowns against all those who have courage to oppose the regime and are fighting for freedom and human dignity; information block-outs; as well as cynical consorting with the world's most dictatorial and criminal regimes, which often get a helping hand from Beijing when the global community tries to do something to put an end to their brutalities (notably, China has never condemned any brutal regime for massacres of its own people or for developing weapons of mass destruction; it always repeats hypocritical calls to resolve issues peacefully and not "to interfere with the internal affairs" of the states where murderers in power are committing violence against their countries' citizens), naturally, cause resentment, anger, and indignation. It is a moral and historical obligation of all democratic states and all honest people in the world who care about justice, the rule of law, morality, and individual freedoms to do their best to send the Chinese leadership a clear message about it.

On the other hand, values, ideals, and emotions are not the right starting point when your task is to analyze the logic of the evolution of the country's political system.

And here the truth is that China is approaching the task of changing its political system in the very same way it has approached the task of economic reforms: gradual, evolutionary, but persistent. Its ruling elite is really trying to find workable answers to key and very difficult questions, while avoiding, by all means, any abrupt revolutionary change.

Let us recollect some major stages of China's political evolution in the post-Mao era.

At the dawn of the market reforms, Deng Xiaoping proclaimed that everything which is good for a human being is socialism, that it is not so important if a cat is black or white as long as it catches mice, and that there is no problem with some Chinese becoming rich earlier than the others. A variety of forms of ownership was allowed, which gave a boost to private enterprise.

At the beginning of the 2000s, the Communist Party opened the door for businessmen to join its ranks.

At the end of the last decade, President Hu Jintao proclaimed that Chinese citizens had the right to openly tell the authorities about their grievances and that the latter must listen to what they say and seek solutions for the issues they pose.

Also, perhaps, China has become the world leader in terms of the number of high-ranking officials executed for corruption-related crimes.

As far as the country's political system is concerned, currently, besides the CPC, China has eight political parties, though all of them are small and, naturally, recognize the CPC's leadership. There are the Revolutionary Committee of the Kuomintang founded by Kuomintang members who did not escape to Taiwan in 1949; the China Democratic National Construction Association, whose members are mostly entrepreneurs; Zhigondang of China—a party of returned overseas Chinese and their relatives; the Taiwan Democratic Self-Government League of prominent people from Taiwan or of Taiwanese heritage now residing in the mainland; and several parties formed by intellectuals: the China Democratic League, the China Association for Promoting Democracy, the China Peasants' and Workers' Party, and the Juisan Society.

At present the Communist leadership openly says that China is not going to step on the path of ideological and political pluralism. However, it does not necessarily mean that in the foreseeable future China's party politics will not undergo any change. Mentioning political reforms by the authorities, even in the negative, is important as such.

Again, the change will be not abrupt: from one party rule to full-fledged multiparty politics, but evolutionary and very gradual. Perhaps, in this decade China will start moving ahead, taking one small step after another, toward a more pluralistic, or rather quasi-pluralistic, political structure. Parties other than the CPC will be gradually given a bit more say and become more noticeable on the domestic political arena, albeit within narrow limits. At a certain point, free elections will be announced, with great pomp. Candidates from various parties will run, but the CPC will surely win with more than 90 percent of the votes and will use it as a proof of the legitimacy of its rule. Other parties (probably they will even be called opposition parties) may be allowed to organize meetings and various public gatherings, but will stop short of criticizing the ruling party too strongly because otherwise they may face tough penalties—for example, for disturbing the social order.

In the CPC-controlled media there will be more and more publications critical of a particular party boss or state bureaucrat, a particular local CPC committee, local government, or the state ministry; or even of certain aspects of the economic and social situation in the country in general. Actually, it would be safe to say that this is already the case: Self-criticism is aptly integrated into the mechanism of preserving and consolidating the CPC power base. Perhaps, at a certain point, the CPC will even move to separate, technically, the functions of the party and the government and gradually eliminate the system of party committees at the enterprises.

In other words, the major trend is and will be a shift from an out-dated communist dictatorship of the traditional type to a more sophis-ticated political system with a democratic facade, but in reality tightly controlled by the CPC ruling elite. The latter may use it to look more legitimate in the eyes of world public opinion or at least to argue that it is legitimate and that it cares about democracy.

In short, China is most likely to undergo a shift to a system for-mally pluralistic/democratic but essentially authoritarian—a system where the change of the ruling party is still effectively impossible. Look around and you will see: There are a lot of countries that can serve as an example.

Chapter 14

Global Rebalancing Will Not Be Easy

C hina's impressive economic performance in the years of the global, or rather Western, downturn resulted first and foremost from its structural and macroeconomic strength.

The role of domestic demand was particularly important. A dramatic plunge of exports was largely offset by an increase in investment and dynamism of private consumption, both supported by the 4 trillion yuan government stimulus package. Similar developments could be traced in India, Indonesia, Vietnam, and a number of other large developing economies.

Decoupling raised expectations about the global economy rebalancing in the postdownturn period.

Can the Idea Work?

The global economy rebalancing idea, advocated by President Obama and other Western leaders and actively promoted by the IMF, is based on the presumption that Americans and Europeans should increase their savings, while the Chinese (as well as people in other large emerging countries) should save less, consume more, and, apparently, buy more Western products. This allegedly will help to get over or at least to substantially reduce global trade imbalances, especially China's surplus and America's deficit. China's abnormally huge foreign exchange reserves will also decrease. The Chinese government is urged to encourage household consumption in various ways including the appreciation of the yuan and development of the social security system. The stronger yuan will reduce prices for imported consumer products. Better social safety nets will make Chinese families more confident in their future and enable them to redirect part of their incomes from savings to consumption.

Can the idea work?

Our answer is that, though step-by-step, certain things will change in the directions described, the probability of the elimination or even reduction of today's China-related global trade imbalances is close to zero. Don't expect too much. Also, the changes counted upon, especially a further spurt of private consumption in China, may have substantial negative side effects and therefore should not be encouraged too strongly.

After all, maybe, what we call today's global imbalances may in fact represent a kind of global equilibrium.

Private Consumption in China Is Already Growing Fast

It is often indicated that the share of private consumption in China's GDP is unusually low. It is true. Furthermore, it has been significantly declining: from 50.6 percent in 1990 to 46.2 percent in 2000 and to 35.7 percent in 2009. In the United States, the ratio is about 70 percent.

However, it would be wrong to forget that in absolute terms China's private consumption has been rising quite fast through most of the market reforms period, especially in the 2000s. Boosted by a double-digit annual increase of wages and household incomes, growth of retail sales averaged 13.6 percent between 2001 and 2008, reaching 16.8 percent in 2007 and 21.6 percent in 2009. In 2009, the Chinese consumed 2.7 times more in nominal and 2.2 times more in real terms (author's calculations based on ADB 2011) than in 2000. The private consumption share of the GDP has been falling simply because other components of final demand, namely capital formation and net exports, have been growing even faster.

Yes, with the further rise of incomes and the expansion of the social security network, Chinese households are likely to save a smaller portion of what they earn, spending more on buying goods and services, and the appreciating yuan will enable them to purchase more foreign-made products.

However, as far as the global economy rebalancing is concerned, this is not the end of the story.

All through the reform decades China's major growth driver—more important than exports—was domestic capital formation, or investment in production machines, factory, and office buildings, as well as in housing construction. In this sense, its growth is already led by domestic demand more than by exports. (As discussed in Part One, China's dynamic and large-scale capital formation as such brings about a significant expansion of its domestic market, but American and European exporters have not taken advantage of these opportunities.) However, up till now, a significant portion of consumer goods produced with those machines at those factories, was exported to America and Europe. Hence, domestic capital formation was very closely linked to and decisively depended on Western-bound exports of consumer goods.

The global downturn years brought an important change: As exports dwindled, a greater part of made-in-China consumer products started to be sold domestically. Even in 2009, real private consumption increased more than 8 percent.

China is going through a long wave of private consumption growth, which started in the 1980s. The wave did not roll back during the global downturn, proving to be an internal affair, unrelated to the ups and downs of Western economies. This was also the case in a number of other large developing countries (Tselichtchev 2010).

Families ascending from the low to the middle-income bracket are usually increasing their consumption at the highest pace. Since hundreds of millions of Chinese households—especially in the central and western provinces, and most of all in small townships and rural areas—still have to make a real big leap forward (not a contrived one like under Mao Zedong in the 1950s) from have-nots to haves, and since, as mentioned in Part One, a significant portion of Chinese middle-class families are still not middle class by Western standards, this wave will continue for decades to come, enabling China to grow even in times when Western economies stumble.

Decoupling is not a temporary phenomenon. It is a new structural feature of the global economy.

Yet Expansion of China's Domestic Demand Is One Thing, and Rebalancing Is Another

However, the growing role of domestic demand, especially private consumption, as China's growth driver, will not necessarily lead to the expected rebalancing of the global economy, at least in the foreseeable future.

There are several reasons.

First, the China-West gap in the scale of private consumption is still too big. Annual private consumption in the United States equals about $10 trillion, in the four largest economies of the euro-zone (Germany, France, Italy, and Spain) $5.6 trillion, in Japan $3.0 trillion. In China, it is only $1.8 trillion (World Bank 2011; all the data is for 2009). Even if the miracle happens and within a short period of time the yuan appreciates against the dollar 1.5 times, it will be no more than some $2.7 trillion. Obviously, it is not enough to make up for the fall or a slowdown of private consumption in the West. And even if private consumption in other large developing countries is added, the picture will not change significantly (in 2009, private consumption amounted to, for example, $771 billion in India, $590 billion in Mexico, and $306 billion in Indonesia).

Second, acceleration of private consumption growth in China will not necessarily lead to a substantial increase of its imports from the United States or Europe. To conquer the Chinese market, Western exporters have to fight really hard, and the outcome of this fight is not at all predetermined. As Part One shows, Chinese firms do not think twice to catch the new opportunities their domestic market opens, and, as an exporter to China, Asia has been doing better than the West. On their part, to establish their presence in China, more and more American and European companies choose to produce locally rather than to export. Therefore Western exporters' ability to capture a substantial portion of the expanding Chinese market is questionable.

Perhaps the easiest way for the West to increase its exports to China in the short run is to promote big deals at the government level—the way the Obama administration did during the U.S.-China Summit in January 2011, when it initiated large-scale contracts to sell airplanes, power-generating machinery, locomotives, and so on. However, this can be done only on a case-by-case basis and is unlikely to change the overall picture of the West-China trade.

Third, the fall of saving rates and the rise of the propensity to consume (consumption share of the disposal income) on the Chinese side and the reverse change in the West, even if this latter change becomes a permanent trend, will not necessarily restrain China's exports to America and Europe. On the one hand, Chinese industries are quite capable of increasing sales at home and in the West simultaneously. China's investment efficiency (value added per unit of investment), which is currently still low by international standards is steadily growing, making it possible to achieve larger output with smaller investment and, consequently, savings. On the other hand if, along the lines of the global rebalancing concept, Western households restrain their purchases of consumer goods in order to save more, the sales of simpler and cheaper goods for everyday use imported from China will suffer less than those of higher-end products manufactured at American and European factories.

That is why, even if both in China and in the West savings and consumption ratios change in the desired direction, rebalancing is unlikely to happen soon and, furthermore, may not become a major trend at all.

Let us not forget that back in the late 1980s, the United States, with the help of its major allies, already made a desperate attempt to rebalance the global economy (though the term rebalancing was not used at that time). It tried to reduce its trade deficit by abruptly appreciating the yen and depreciating the dollar in the hope that Japan, which had the largest trade surplus at that time, would consume and import more and export less. In September 1985 the meeting in New York of finance ministers and central bank chiefs of the five major industrial nations produced the Plaza Accord on a joint intervention in the foreign exchange markets. As a result the average annual exchange rate of the yen against the dollar soared from 200.6 yen to $1 in 1985 to 160.1 yen in 1986 and to 122.0 yen in 1987 (Tselichtchev and Debroux 2009). However, even in the wake of such a dramatic appreciation, Japan's exports stumbled only for a little more than a year and began to rapidly increase again from 1987. Japan dynamically expanded *both* domestic consumption and exports, and, after all, the U.S. deficit in the bilateral trade continued to beat one record after another.

At that time, in the golden years of the Japanese economy, Japan's exports were not stopped by the currency appreciation due to very high nonprice competitiveness of its companies and their ability to differentiate products. Today's China is still far from that level of nonprice competitiveness. However, it has more than enough bargaining power not to allow a rapid appreciation of its currency, and controls global markets of many products as a dominant producer/exporter. Thus, it is also in a very good position to retain and further expand its trade surplus.

Too Rapid Increase of China's Consumption May Have Dire Side Effects

To change the angle, it is important to keep in mind that too rapid growth of private consumption by the 1.3 billion Chinese may have negative side effects for China itself and for the whole world, by far offsetting achievements in terms of rebalancing: a further strain on the natural environment; shortages of energy and mineral resources, food and other products; and exacerbating global inflation.

For instance, the 2000s were marked by a very rapid increase of Chinese households' consumption of food—largely because tens if not hundreds of millions of Chinese could afford to have three meals a day instead of two. This is a natural and positive change. It should be so. However, even this natural and positive change pushed up global demand for foodstuffs and became a major factor of food inflation, which started from around 2006, was interrupted by the global downturn, and came back again as soon as it was over.

China has already become the largest automobile market in the world, but I would feel relieved if the Chinese stop short of reaching Western levels of motorization and car ownership by families, in order to preserve the environment and also not to make life in the big and not so big cities a nightmare.

The Chinese will have to think of, and maybe even propose to the world, patterns of consumption alternative to those established in the West—at least to the ones adopted by the West when it was at the stage of economic development similar to the one China is going through now. These patterns have to be more environment-friendly, take into account natural resources constraints, and, for these reasons, wisely restrain the scale of consumption of particular products and services, avoiding Western-style consumption excesses.

As for Chinese families' savings and the country's huge foreign exchange reserves, their reduction, especially a substantial reduction, may harm the West rather than benefit it. The reason is obvious: They are supporting Western nations in times of the worst public debt crisis in their modern history.

Don't push the rebalancing idea too hard.

Present Position: Imbalance or Equilibrium?

It could be better to adjust the angle somewhat.

Contrary to conventional wisdom, today's China-West trade and economic relationship *does* provide for a certain kind of global equilibrium. It may be far from optimal, especially from the West's point of view, but it is not as bad as how you feel when you read numerous publications in the Western media or listen to politicians' speeches.

Here is the equilibrium's outline.

Chinese households' large savings are translating into a high investment rate (ratio of domestic investment to the GDP), rapid growth of production, and increasing exports to the West. Earning a lot of foreign currency, China boosts its foreign reserves (they expand further as Chinese monetary authorities buy foreign currencies to keep the yuan weak). The reserves are used to purchase Western securities, first of all U.S. Treasury bonds and other government debt. Today it helps the United States and other Western governments fight with budget deficits and ease the pain of deep public spending cuts.

It is an imbalance for the United States and the West in general, as well as for China—as long as we look upon them as separate players. However, it becomes a sort of equilibrium if we look on the global economy as an entity, with national economies as its integral parts.

For decades, America's enormous current account deficits were the focus of attention of economists, policy makers, and the media. All through those decades, critics and skeptics did not stop saying that they were unsustainable. However, in reality they have proved to be quite *sustainable*: The U.S. economy remains safe as long as the inflow of capital continues and the capital and financial account remains in a comfortable black. Running large trade and current account deficits, the United States played the role of the major market creator for the world, supporting global growth, including growth in countries that were its major creditors. It was and is kind of a deal: market for money.

Having become the U.S. government's major creditor, Beijing is and will be committed to playing its part because economic stability of America is indispensable for China itself: The United States is one of its most important trading partners.

Furthermore, China is becoming an increasingly important creditor not only for the United States, but also for European countries. About one-fourth of its total foreign reserves have been invested in euro-denominated assets (Reuter 2011). Without any doubt, Beijing will be playing an increasingly important role in saving the heavily indebted European governments of Greece, Portugal, Spain, Italy, and so on from the financial fiasco and in supporting the euro.

It is noticeably increasing the purchases of Japanese securities as well. In 2010, their amount was 27 times greater than a year earlier, exceeding 21 trillion yen (the average for 2005–2009 was only 1 trillion yen). Most of this China money was invested in short-term Japanese government bonds, but purchases of long-term government debt also doubled reaching almost 470 billion yen. China became the fifth-largest investor in Japanese securities after the United Kingdom, France, the United States, and Hong Kong, while a year earlier it was only at number 17 (Nikkei 2011a).

To repeat, this kind of China-West equilibrium is far from perfect and is not the one the West desires. For China it is a trump card giving it growing political and diplomatic leverage. However, today this imperfect equilibrium is real and basically workable for all the parties involved, while the global rebalancing idea is more like a castle made of sand.

As of 2010–2011, it is becoming more and more obvious that the global recovery brings back precrisis patterns of economic growth and international trade (in the first chapter of Part Three we look at this issue from a different angle showing that these patterns match the interests of the Chinese leadership).

In 2010, the U.S. economy grew 3.0 percent. Growth was driven first of all by private consumption, which, in the last quarter, increased 4.4 percent year-on-year, contributing 3 percentage points to the total increment of the GDP (Willis 2011). The merchandise trade deficit soared 27.5 percent to $645.1 billion from $ 505.9 billion a year earlier (Bureau of Economic Analysis 2011b). The deficit in trade with China reached $273.1 billion, or 42 percent of the total. Imports from China hit the record of $364.9 billion (U.S. Census Bureau 2011b).

Annual growth of the EU-27 countries was 1.8 percent (IMF 2011), but in the fourth quarter it accelerated to 2.2 percent (Trading Economics 2010). EU imports from China rose 31 percent to 281.9 billion euro. Exports were less than half that amount: 113.1 billion euro, or 38 percent more than in 2009 (EC Commission 2011).

As the global downturn was over, America and Europe began to expand private consumption and imports again. Meanwhile, China's growth again became increasingly export-led as the expansion of its domestic demand slowed down because of the monetary policy tightening and a receding impact of the economic stimulus.

There is still room to maintain this kind of China-West economic relationship.

In the wake of the crisis, American and European households have begun to save more. However it does not mean that in the post-crisis period their saving rates will continue elevating. On the contrary, as the economy gradually improves, they will seek to restore their pre-crisis consumption patterns (though downward pressures on incomes, employment concerns, and tougher constraints on consumer credit will restrain the consumption growth pace). It will drive their propensity to consume up and saving rates down, though apparently not to the bottom levels of the previous decade.

On the other hand, the Chinese, as well as most other Asians, will continue to boost their savings—especially as the central banks will be raising policy interest rates to contain soaring inflation and prevent overheating.

Consequently, China's trade surplus and the West's trade deficits will be expanding again.

For the period between 2011 and 2016, the IMF predicts a steady decline of saving rates in the euro zone and in the United Kingdom, and a V-shaped change in the United States and Japan. In the United States, the rates are expected to fall until 2013 and rise again to about 6 percent in 2016. On the other hand, within the same period, savings in developing Asia are predicted to increase by about 1.25 points of GDP. According to the forecast, China's current account surplus will hit a new record of $454.6 billion in 2016 (three times as much as in 2009), while in the five coming years the U.S. current account deficit will rise 1.7 times (IMF 2011).

Don't expect the global economy to be radically rebalanced in the foreseeable future.

Conclusions

First, the global financial and economic crisis of 2008–2009 was not really global. It was Western, just as the crisis of 1997–1998 was mostly Asian. Times have changed: Western economies are already not big enough to trigger global crises by their failures. China, along with other large emerging economies, was not in crisis.

Second, the crisis manifested the failure of the Western model of capitalism. Namely, it failed to enable responsible behavior on the part of many households on the one hand and financiers on the other. The former boosted their consumption beyond affordable levels. The latter went on a lending spree and got increasingly engaged in risky financial gambling. The supermen of the financial world (at least they seemed to be supermen) playing with structured instruments on a tremendous scale and at a very high risk, became the heroes of the decade, keeping hostage entire national economies and the fates of millions of people. They did not bear adequate responsibility for the fiasco they engineered.

Neither state supervision nor proper corporate governance was in place to prevent all these abnormalities. The real face of Western capitalism proved to be quite different from its established image.

Third, the most natural solutions for the problems the crisis has posed are more reasonable consumption patterns, prudent management, higher transparency and stronger accountability of financial institutions, and better state supervision. The Western model of capitalism (both its Anglo-Saxon and continental European versions) has to be repaired. However, Western countries do not need a shift to any kind of state capitalism or a different economic system. Nationalizations and bailouts were a temporary, mostly short-term emergency step.

Fourth, though the crisis of 2008–2009 is over, its long shadow is still there. Its legacy will haunt Western economies for years to come, making the recovery slow and incomplete.

As a punishment for financial adventurism of the precrisis years, most Western countries have to fight with unprecedented public debts, and in a cohort of European states the sovereign debt crisis has reached a critical stage, effectively making government bonds a questionable asset and undermining the confidence toward financial institutions possessing them.

The public finance troubles make the West accelerate the painful process of trimming the welfare state.

As business confidence remains low, the recovery does not translate into a significant number of new jobs. The unemployment rate in the United States has hit the European levels of about 10 percent.

At the same time, inflation risks are on the rise. Inflationary effects of the public spending spree and loosened monetary policy of 2008– 2009 will be felt for quite a long period of time, coupled with the impact of the increase in the global prices for fuels, mineral resources, and food. Some Western economies are already coming under strong inflationary pressures at a very early stage of the recovery and amid a very sluggish growth. In other words, stagflation is knocking at the door.

Fifth, in relative terms, the crisis of 2008–2009 made China stronger and the West weaker.

It happened not only because the Chinese economy was growing while Western economies stumbled. The key point is that China proved to be immune to the structural diseases the West failed to contain. Furthermore, learning from the West's negative experience, it is taking preventive measures not to catch these diseases in the future.

Structurally, today's China is stronger than most Western economies.

Sixth, China's Communist regime has shown a remarkable ability to address the country's major problems step-by-step, in an evolutionary way.

China is not facing a threat of a political turmoil like the one in Eastern and Central Europe in the late 1980s through the early 1990s or in the Middle East in 2011. The reason is that, unlike the countries of those regions, in China the leadership is really trying, in its own way, to address people's grievances and propose solutions (albeit they are often far from perfect). The country's political system is not stagnating, but undergoing a Chinese-style evolutionary change. There is a lot of room for further gradual evolution: toward a society with a more pluralistic political façade, but with the CPC remaining in power and unchallenged by any other political force.

Seventh, the economic system of today's China is not state capitalism as opposed to Western capitalism with private entrepreneurship at its core.

It is a state-private capitalism where the position of the private sector is gradually getting stronger. Competition in China is usually fiercer than in the West. As time goes by, Chinese capitalism integrates more and more elements of conventional Western capitalism, combining them with its own specific features such as a key role for market-style SOEs. The mix of Western and non-Western features is a factor of China's economic strength.

Eighth, rebalancing of the global economy through China's shift from savings to consumption and from export-led to domestic demand-led growth and Western economies' shift in the opposite direction will be difficult.

As time goes by, the Chinese will be saving less and consuming more, and this will result in larger imports. However, it can hardly become a major road to global rebalancing in the foreseeable future. The scale of private consumption in China is still incomparable with that in the West. Western exporters' ability to capture significant shares of the expanding Chinese market is questionable. Finally, even if Western consumers spend more cautiously, it will not necessarily restrain imports of made-in-China goods.

There is a different kind of global economic equilibrium already in place, and it is likely to be preserved for years to come. Growing, further increasing its exports to the West and recirculating the money it earns, China is financing the West's budget deficits, and also gradually increasing direct investment to the United States, Europe, and Japan, helping to invigorate local industries and create jobs.

Also, though a developing country itself, the new economic giant is in a good position to further increase its contribution to development aid all around the world.

Part Three

THE CHINA-WEST ECONOMIC WARS: AND THE WINNER IS. . . .

C hina and the West are at an economic war going on at several fronts. It is the war for dominance and wealth between the political establishments and business elites. It is also the fight to survive, involving myriads of small and medium businesses on both sides and hundreds of millions of ordinary working guys.

It is one of the strangest wars in world history. Both sides are fighting at full strength, but unlike previous wars, even economic, neither side wants the rival to suffer a complete defeat. Neither China, nor the West seeks to economically weaken the counterpart so that the latter would have to leave the battlefield as happened, for example, in the case of the West and the former Soviet Union.

China and the West need one another, like two boxers or two rival soccer teams. China needs the rich, economically and socially stable, and technologically-progressive West, and the West needs dynamic, cash-abundant China. In this economic war, the victory matters and makes sense only if the rival remains sufficiently healthy and strong and keeps on running. Too heavy a blow for one side becomes a blow for another, too. Thus, naturally, the two sides are not only fighting, but also interacting and supporting each other in various ways.

Yet, the China-West economic war is real. One of its major dimensions is the fight for the position making it possible to determine the rules of conduct on the global economic arena and the ways key international issues are approached.

As time goes by, the situation on the battlefield tends to change in China's favor.

Within a very short period of time, it has developed tremendous bargaining power: the power to push its own interest on the global stage and to make others accept or at least reconcile themselves to its point of view. This bargaining power, though absolutely nonquantifiable, exerts decisive influence on how key international economic issues are handled. The West often lacks the tools and means to address the challenge.

Chapter 15

China's Choice Is to Further Expand Trade Surpluses and Keep the Yuan Weak

The major China-West economic battlefield is foreign trade and the yuan exchange rate policy.

The Rationale for Not Appreciating the Yuan Faster

The United States and other Western powers are pressing China hard to reduce its trade surplus by allowing the yuan to appreciate at a higher speed. They argue that it will not only correct the trade imbalances, but also serve the interests of China itself, making its imports cheaper, households richer, private consumption greater, and inflation lower.

Dropping the demand for a faster yuan appreciation would be an act of diplomatic insanity.

Nevertheless, obviously, China will continue appreciating the yuan at its own turtle's pace, rejecting the demands to speed up. As a result, its huge trade surpluses will not decline, but, on the contrary, expand even further.

The West's and China's sets of priorities are different.

America and Europe are nervous about trade imbalances. In contrast, the Chinese side feels very comfortable with the undervalued yuan as it helps it to remain in command of the world's major markets and guarantees growth of exporting industries. This is an advantage that is not easily given away, irrespective of what Chinese officials are saying about their readiness to reduce the surplus.

The West says that the yuan appreciation will benefit Chinese consumers making affordable a wider range of goods from around the world.

This is correct. The hurdle, however, is that in today's China, due to its phenomenal growth uninterrupted for an exceptionally long period of time, households' living standards are elevating fast even with the undervalued national currency—first of all due to the increase in the consumption of domestically made products. In this sense, both Chinese consumers and Chinese producers turn out to be beneficiaries—a really nice combination.

Another crucial point is that, keeping the yuan weak, Chinese authorities send a clear message to Western manufacturers: "Why bother exporting? Better come here and produce in China!" And, with really few alternatives left (in case they want to be cost-competitive, of course), a growing number of Western companies choose to produce locally rather than to export, strengthening China's production and export power even further. Moreover, as time goes by, they transfer to China increasingly advanced technologies and establish state-of-the-art R&D facilities (see the following section). A weak yuan is a tool of not only trade, but also investment policy. It is used to bring in the best companies from around the world.

The Rationale for Increasing Savings and Exports Rather than Consumption

The West makes its demands: Switch to demand-led domestic growth! Save less and consume more!

However, irrespective of what government officials are saying, the Chinese side is not so eager to rapidly shift in this direction either. An expansionary, demand-boosting macroeconomic policy increases the asset bubble risk. In China's case, if this risk is not carefully managed, a consecutive bubble burst may bring an economic, social, and political disaster. Once the global downturn is over, overseas markets are by and large getting back to normal and inflationary pressures are mounting. The safest way for the Chinese leadership is not to stimulate private consumption and domestic demand in general, but to cool them down through a tighter monetary policy, again relying on exports as the major growth driver. (It will change if the West's financial and economic troubles worsen again.)

High savings also remain a very important factor of China's economic strength, and also of social stability. On the one hand, they strengthen Chinese families' confidence in their future. On the other, they support large-scale investment and steady production growth needed to create jobs. Though investment is somewhat restrained by a deflationary macroeconomic policy, it is still growing fast, as exports are robust.

To summarize, in spite of all the external diplomatic pressures, under present conditions (and unless the West falls into a new recession), the China of the early 2010s still chooses to continue with mostly investment/export-led growth rather than to switch to growth led by households' consumption.

This growth pattern continues to boost its foreign reserves, enhancing Beijing's role as the West's major creditor. For the Chinese political establishment it is also good news, because the creditor position makes it easier to persuade the counterparts to accept China's rules of the game, not only on economic issues.

This is a really big political game. For the country's rulers it is far more important than giving Chinese families a chance to live better with a stronger yuan and wider access to overseas products.

Chapter 16

Environment: China Going Its Own Way

Environment represents one more major area where Chinese and Western interests clash.

China has become the world's number one polluter. According to some estimates, as of 2007, it emitted 14 percent more greenhouse gases than the United States (Asia Society's Center on U.S.-China Relations 2009).

At the global climate change talks held within the UN Framework Convention on Climate Change (UNFCCC), the West has been urging Beijing to set binding numerical targets for the reduction of its carbon dioxide emissions as part of the post-Kyoto Protocol global deal. China, naturally, disagrees and, along with other developing nations, insists on a fundamentally different approach.

Overall, a lot of doubts remain about the way today's key environmental issues are addressed at the global level.

Global Climate Talks: Doubts Remain If Not Increase

To begin with, the relevance of the UNFCCC talks themselves looks questionable. There is a strong impression that they have been hastily arranged, poorly prepared, and based on doubtful premises.

Their goal is to cut the emissions of carbon dioxide in order to keep the global temperature increase within at least two degrees Celsius compared to the preindustrial period. However, there is still no clear and internationally accepted scientific evidence that emission of CO_2 is the major factor of global warming—on the contrary, recently we hear a lot of arguments against this assumption. Even some prominent champions of the fight with CO_2, beginning with Al Gore, have openly admitted that it may not be so. The data published by experts including James Hansen, director of NASA's Goddard Institute for Space Studies and "the grandfather of the global warming theory," shows that gases other than CO_2 are responsible for most—and currently maybe even for all—of the global warming, and that the major greenhouse gas is methane. Furthermore, there is a lot of skepticism about global warming alarmism as such.

The negotiations framework based on shaky presumptions is doubtful by definition. At least it would be safe to say that, to draw a sound conclusion on whether the road that has been chosen is right or not, much more preliminary scientific work has to be done.

However, not surprisingly, once the UN talk machine has started, it cannot be stopped.

The talks are held by diplomats—professional negotiators engaged in usual diplomatic bargaining about who has to cut the CO_2 emissions by how much and on what conditions. The aim is to achieve an annual emissions reduction totaling 40–44 billion tons by 2020, considered necessary to contain the temperature rise within two degrees. Current reduction pledges by the countries involved leave a gap of 10–14 billion tons.

At the ministerial conference in Cancun, Mexico, in December 2010, developed countries submitted their numerical reduction targets, and 48 developing states presented information on the national appropriate mitigation actions (NAMAs) they intend to take in their effort to deviate, as far as the emissions are concerned, from business as usual by 2020. These actions, however, are conditioned on the West's technological and financial support. The agreement was reached on the establishment of Green Climate Fund, of the Adaptation Committee to support countries as they compile climate protection plans, and of the Technology Mechanism.

Difficult talks will go on and on, but the key issue of the reduction levels and the reduction format for every particular country will obviously remain unsettled as long as the West repeats its claims that it cannot do it alone without China, India, and other large developing nations making mandatory cuts of their own. The latter will argue that they cannot accept binding obligations because they have the right to develop and that, as the problem itself was caused by the industrial development of the West, it is exactly the West that has to take the major responsibility for the emissions cuts.

The possibility that China will yield to the West's pressure and come out with internationally binding CO_2 reduction targets is zero. Zero in principle, in any case—even if in China such reductions were not associated with unacceptable sacrifices in terms of growth and development (in reality they are). China basically seeks to avoid assuming obligations that make it accountable to supranational institutions, especially if their agenda is articulated predominantly by Western powers.

The climate talks are showing, first, the West's inability to get any meaningful concessions from Beijing and, second, China's strong bargaining power, enabling it to address the problems in its own way and at its own pace. In this sense, it is similar to the yuan appreciation issue.

The Cancun conference has clarified the contours of the formula for a possible compromise if any compromise at all is achievable. Developed countries will have to reduce their emissions in absolute terms on a mandatory basis. Developing countries will make reductions on a voluntary basis, mostly targeting the levels of emissions per unit of the GDP. The West will have to support those reductions financially and technically—by the way, allocating a lot of funds in times when its own finances are in disarray. This is it—a very asymmetric deal. A more favorable combination for the West is hardly feasible.

If a scheme of this kind is launched, the West will bear the heaviest environmental burden in terms of both reduction levels and financing.

Concern about the Impact on Growth

Definitely, it looks better not to hurry too much with the launch of this scheme.

Along with more research on CO_2 and other pollutants' contribution to global warming and, maybe, on the danger of global warming as such, it is vital to have a deeper look at and put a stronger emphasis on the relationship between emission cuts on the one hand and economic growth and people's lives on the other.

A few think tanks, especially in Europe, have published very optimistic estimates about the effects these cuts will have on economic growth and employment, emphasizing the role of investment in an array of environment-friendly industries. The tough reality, however, is that, though opening a range of new business opportunities, emission cuts will also force both households and industries to make sacrifices. And it looks very strange that the UN-sponsored talks are based just on the calculations of the CO_2 emissions cuts necessary to keep the temperature rise within two degrees, while detailed estimates of the effects those cuts will have on the countries' economic growth and development, employment, consumption, and living standards are not on the table.

As far as China is concerned, no one on the Western side seems to bother to take into account that, for example, absolute emissions cuts may cause a really serious slowdown in the Chinese economy, posing the risk of a social explosion—a revolt of hundreds of millions of people deprived of any real chance they had to overcome poverty and rise from primitive to modern lifestyles.

Let us not forget that the lion's share of China's emissions is accounted for by industries (the steel industry alone emits more than all Chinese households combined), while emissions by households are very low by international standards—simply because the modernization of consumption patterns and lifestyles is still at an early stage. On the contrary, in the United States industries account for only 25 percent of the total emissions, while most of the rest comes from transportation, commercial, and residential use. On a per capita basis, China emits 78 percent less than the United States (Asia Society's Center on U.S.-China Relations 2009), and emissions by an average urban Chinese household are estimated to still be around one-third those by an average household in the West (Tselichtchev & Debroux 2009). Rural households emit much less.

Also, surprisingly, Western negotiators are not much concerned about the fact that imposition of too harsh emission constraints on China, the main engine of today's global growth, may have negative consequences for the West itself, as China's slowdown will squeeze the most dynamically expanding market, crucially important sources of many products' supply, and, after all, one of the major channels of financing of Western governments and businesses.

A Wider Angle Is Needed

To address environmental challenges of our time, it is crucial to overcome existing global stereotypes and think of alternative approaches.

The time is ripe to go far beyond the UNFCCC framework (though it doesn't mean a call to bury it altogether) and, first of all, to make it clear that today's environmental issues should be looked upon from a much wider angle than the one of the climate change talks. We are facing a really big global problem of *the deterioration of the natural environment* on our Mother Earth, which includes deforestation, extinction of many species of plants and animals, air pollution, water contamination, more and more frequent extreme weather events, unbearable noise levels in the cities, and so on. Obviously, the problem is not limited to CO_2 emissions or rising temperatures.

Every country or groups of countries must do their utmost to find and implement the solutions taking into account their development stage, economic and social conditions, financial and technological capabilities, and so on. Comprehensive environmental solutions have to be well balanced with policies and measures aimed at achieving other key social and economic goals. Countries should actively exchange information and experience in this area, launch joint projects (both at the bilateral and multilateral level) where possible, and set binding or nonbinding environmental targets for themselves if they consider them useful.

The UN should not be looked upon as the only coordinator of international efforts—furthermore, it is unlikely to be the most efficient coordinator.

Definitely, the West should actively assist developing countries working to preserve and improve their natural environment—financially, technologically, and intellectually. However, it has to be made clear that, especially in the area of financing, limits exist as most Western economies themselves are facing tough fiscal constraints. Apparently, with its huge foreign exchange reserves, China could and should accept the role of one of the major sources of global environmental financing.

China's Pro-Environmental Drive

Focusing on the China-West conflicts of interest that surfaced at the UNFCCC talks, we may well overlook a very simple fact of fundamental importance. The Chinese side fully recognizes the current critical state of the country's natural environment and is already taking drastic steps to protect and improve it, thus contributing a lot to the global environment protection effort.

First of all, China has pledged to cut by 2020 its carbon dioxide emissions per unit of GDP by 40–45 percent below the 2005 level: quite an ambitious goal for a rapidly growing and a very energy-intensive economy.

In June 2004, the government announced a Medium- and Long-Term Energy Plan for 2005–2020, and, based on it, in November the same year the National Development and Reform Commission put together the energy conservation plan for the same period.

For the 11th Five-Year Plan period (2006–2010), the target for the reduction of primary energy consumption in standard coal per unit of GDP was set at 20 percent (in reality, by 2009 it was reduced by 14.38 percent according to the Chinese government and by a little more than 8.2 percent according to an alternative estimate [Howes 2010]), and for the reduction of water consumption per unit of industry value-added at 30 percent (this target was achieved). The total emission of the two big pollutants, sulfur dioxide and chemical oxygen demand (COD), had to be cut by 10 percent.

The government started to set mandatory energy conservation targets for local administrations, and meeting those targets was included in the criteria for the evaluation of their performance. For China, where the major criteria had been the achieved rate of economic growth, it was a substantial step forward.

According to the latest data available at the time of writing, the five-year target on the reduction of the pollutants' emissions was exceeded. Also, according to the Ministry of Environmental Protection, within those five years, a total of 500 million kilowatts of desulfurization facilities in coal-fired power plants (coal-fired power plants cover about 80 percent of China's total electric power needs) were built, and the urban sewage treatment rate at the end of the period rose to 75 percent against 52 percent in 2005 (*China Daily* 2011).

In the 12th Five-Year Plan (2011–2015) two more major pollutants, nitrogen oxide and ammonia nitrogen, have been added to the pollution reduction targets. Within five coming years, per unit of GDP, carbon dioxide emission has to be reduced by 17 percent and energy consumption by 16 percent (APCO Worldwide 2010).

In 2009, a special state supervision system was introduced for companies consuming energy and water beyond the government-set limits.

The Law on Renewable Energy amended in 2010 established the system of state purchase guarantees for renewable energy producers and set the stage for the creation of the state-financed Renewable Energy Development Fund to subsidize electric power companies buying renewable energy but not covering their purchasing costs by the sales of electricity (Tsuchiya 2010).

In early 2011, Chinese academics and experts articulated a three-step goal to curb pollution in the next 40 years. The first step has to be made by 2020; its aim is to achieve control over the emission of major pollutants and to ensure the nation's environmental safety. The second phase will continue until 2030 when the emissions volume of all pollutants will be under full control and improvement will have been made in "overall environmental quality." Finally, by the end of 2050, the environmental quality should be "compatible with people's increasing quality of living for a country that is a modern socialist power" (Xinhua 2011)—or shall we say "to meet the standards of a modern developed country"?

China-West Environmental Cooperation

Going its own way, China has embarked on a large-scale pro-environmental drive, boosting a range of green industries. Supporting this drive is, basically, in the interests of the West and of the whole world. The West should do much more to speed it up.

Joint China-U.S., China-EU, and China-Japan environmental projects, including joint research and development, can be increased in scale. Much more can be done to transfer to China progressive environmental technologies and solutions—not as a development aid, but on a purely commercial basis. China should drastically cut or eliminate tariffs on their imports.

On its part, the West has to clearly articulate the idea that environmental policies should not impede growth—in other words, explicitly recognize China's and other developing countries' right to grow. In this regard, it is more relevant for them to set targets for the reduction of CO_2 emissions per unit of GDP than for absolute reductions. The steps China and other large developing states are going to take in this direction deserve to be strongly supported and not criticized as insufficient.

In 2008, a new start was made in the environmental cooperation between China and the United States. The two sides signed the Decade of Energy and Environmental Cooperation Framework, specifying its five major areas: clean energy, clean water, clean air, clean and efficient transportation, and conservation of forest and wetland systems.

The U.S.-China collaboration on a range of energy and environment issues began about 30 years ago. However, as it is pointed out by the authors of "A Roadmap for U.S.-China Cooperation on Energy and Climate Change," a joint report by Asia Society's Center on U.S.-China Relations and the Pew Center on Global Climate Change,

> Too often . . . cooperation has been miscellaneous and episodic rather than sustained. It has also been undermined by insufficient funding, shifting policy priorities, and failure to significantly "scale-up" promising projects. The cancellation or down-scaling by the United States of key projects have led to understandable skepticism in China on the prospects for stronger long-term cooperation. Recent examples include the expiration and eventual renewal of the U.S.-China Protocol on Energy Efficiency and Renewable Energy and the postponement and significant restructuring of the FutureGEN project

to build a commercial scale advanced generation coal plant with carbon capture and storage. (Asia Society's Center on U.S.-China Relations 2009)

The Roadmap urges Washington and Beijing to start acting in concert immediately to find remedies for greenhouse emissions, without waiting for new domestic legislation or multilateral agreements. It suggests that, as the first step, they should arrange a special summit to launch a new energy and climate change partnership. The key areas are low-emission coal technologies, energy efficiency and conservation, advanced electric grids, renewable energy, and so on.

China and the EU also have an agreement on energy and climate change. Among other things, the two sides are studying the possibility of low carbon economic zones, in line with China's special economic zones (SEZ) promotion policy. Several existing Chinese SEZs are already attracting low-carbon investments. The Tianjin zone is hosting leading wind turbine and solar voltaic manufacturers.

Finally, energy/environment cooperation between China and Japan is the largest in scale and in many respects unique in its contents. In the late 1970s, Japan began to provide to China massive official development assistance (ODA), becoming its number one donor. For Tokyo itself, Beijing was by far the largest aid recipient. Up to 2007, more than 3 trillion yen had been provided in the form of preferential yen loans and 325 billion yen as grants. As time went by, especially since the 1990s, Japan's aid became increasingly focused on energy conservation and the environment. Interestingly, it is continuing until the current period, though at a substantially reduced scale, as it is not easy to find a rationale for aiding the country that has overtaken Japan as the world's second-largest economy. (As far as the economic rationale is concerned, today it would be more relevant for China to extend large-scale loans to Japan to assist it in the post-earthquake reconstruction, but unfortunately there is no hope that either side, especially the Japanese, will show enough creativity, courage, and will to take steps in this direction; instead, Japan is about to embark on new tax hikes, which will further undermine its already weak growth potential.) Among other things, Japan financed such projects as Environment Model Cities in Guiyang, Chongqing, and Dalian; Ningxia Afforestation and Vegetation Cover; Xiang River Basin Hunan Environment Improvement (building a sewage system) project in the Hunan Province; and construction of a sewage treatment plant in Beijing.

In 2006 a new cooperation framework was put into action: Japan–China Energy Conservation and Environment Forums attended by government officials, business leaders, experts, academics, representatives of nonprofit organizations, and so on. These forums produce quite tangible results, giving a start to dozens of new bilateral energy/environmental projects. For example, the Yazaki Corporation and Tianjin Bihai Energy Development Co. Ltd established a joint venture providing energy conservation diagnosis and related technical and management consulting services. Hitachi Appliances signed an agreement with the Shenzhen Coolead Industry for the installation of 8,400 air-conditioning systems for energy-efficient buildings (Maeda 2007). China's Baosteel, Shuogang Group, and Wuhan Iron and Steel have introduced Japanese technologies in the coke dry-quenching (CDQ) process (Xinhua 2007). One of the most successful undertakings was a joint venture between Kawasaki Heavy Industries and the Anhui Couch Venture Investment Company to manufacture boilers for waste heat power generation to be used at cement plants.

At the fifth forum in October 2010, a record 44 cooperation agreements were signed including sludge treatment; water treatment, production, and recycling; and the first agreements on smart grid and smart community projects (METI 2010).

A nexus of bilateral environmental projects carried out by China and leading industrially developed states can bring much more tangible results within much shorter periods of time than complicated and highly politicized multilateral talks.

China as a New World Leader in Green Business?

On the other hand, China is becoming an increasingly strong competitor if not a leader in a range of green business areas from clean energy to electric vehicles.

Currently, these sectors are developing fast under the strong leadership of the state, which is formulating strategies and injecting enormous public funds. China easily dismisses the West's concerns about the state involvement and market-distorting subsidies. It simply says: "You really want us to cut emissions and protect the environment, don't you?" A cohort of state-sponsored Chinese green industries and green companies is emerging at a breathtaking speed, and some of them, as mentioned in Part One, are conquering global markets.

Himin Solar Energy Group produces solar thermal systems over twice the volume of their total annual sales in the United States and is now expanding into photovoltaics and other areas (Norris 2010).

China already has a solar-powered city of Rizhao in the Shandong Province, with a population of around 3 million people, where traffic lights, street lamps, and over 60,000 green houses use solar energy, and 99 percent of the households in the central districts have solar water heaters. It has over 500,000 square meters of solar water heating panels (Levesque 2007).

The Chinese version of the Silicon Valley: Electricity Valley in Baoding has become one of the fastest-growing production platforms for wind and solar energy equipment, housing nearly 200 renewable energy companies.

A new Solar Valley City has now been constructed in Dezhou, Shandong Province, to become a national center for manufacturing, R&D, education, and tourism around solar energy technologies. It is home to about 100 solar enterprises with some 800,000 employees.

Within five years, the total investment in solar energy by China and other Asian nations is expected to exceed that of the United States by more than three times (Norris 2010).

Another representative example of China's emergence as a leader in green business is production of electric vehicles (EVs). The target for 2015 is 500,000 units. By 2020, the number is expected to reach 1 million. China is very much likely to become the world's top EV manufacturer.

Their production is boosted by the national strategy of replacing current public transport vehicles with battery-powered ones. In 2009, 25 Chinese cities joined hands to launch a pilot program to demonstrate the advantages of using EV as a means of public transportation. Since then, as of late 2010, 8.5 billion yuan (about $1.28 billion) has been invested into the program, mostly by venture capitalists and automakers. For its part, the Chinese government provides generous EV subsidies to buyers—perhaps, unthinkable in any other country. In some cases, such subsidy reaches 60 thousand yuan, or $9,035 (Loveday 2010). The total planned amount of government spending on manufacturing and selling the EV in 2011–2015 equals $15 billion (*Want China Times* 2011).

The probability is very high that by the end of this decade China will be a leading green business nation.

Chapter 17

A Fight for Natural Resources: China Sets New Rules of the Game

C hina and the West are fighting for the access to and control over fuel and mineral resources around the world.

Changes in the Global Markets

Global markets of energy and mineral resources are undergoing far-reaching irreversible changes, and so are perceptions about the policies needed to provide their stable supply. Global demand is surging due to a dramatic increase of consumption by the fast-growing large emerging economies. Between 1980 and 2000, China's energy consumption doubled, while its GDP quadrupled. Between 2002 and 2005, on the contrary, its energy consumption was growing faster than the

GDP. The energy demand in the four years prior to 2006 increased more than in the previous quarter-century (Asia Society's Center on U.S.-China Relations 2009).

On the supply side, uncertainties and destabilization risks are exacerbating due to rising political instability in exporting countries, periodical redirections of sales from external to domestic markets by leading suppliers (China itself has shown an example in this regard, cutting exports of rare metals—a key input for high-tech industries, while it accounts for 97 percent of their global supply; other examples include Indonesia's petroleum and natural gas, Russia's petroleum products and timber, and so on), and, to a certain extent, a depletion, in some major producing countries, of existing deposits in the absence of new ones whose discovery and exploitation could make up for the loss.

Therefore, oil and some other natural resources are becoming more and more attractive targets for speculators.

In these circumstances, countries highly dependent on natural resources imports, especially those that don't have their own powerful resource multinationals, get increasingly concerned about supply destabilization risks. Predictions about an all-out resource war or bitter fights among buyers for limited amounts of oil or metallic ores look like an exaggeration. However, buyers' competition for particular kinds of resources within particular periods of time due to particular circumstances is becoming a more frequent phenomenon.

For instance, in the most recent development, the Philippines and Vietnam protested to China against its patrol boats hindering their oil exploration activities near the disputed Spratly Islands in the South China Sea. China demanded that its neighbors stop exploration work in this area. Tensions rose as the United States declared that the South China Sea was in the sphere of its national interest and that it would stand by the Philippines as its ally.

Chinese Model of Tapping Resources

China, already a major importer of fuels and many minerals, is getting equipped for such a competition especially fast: With its rapidly growing, highly energy- and resources-intensive economy, the consequences of resource supply irregularities may be fatal. In the days of the Iraq war Beijing already resorted to eventually a panic buying of petroleum, over-straining the global markets.

In today's world, to avoid supply troubles, it is considered preferable to establish long-term relationships with particular resource-rich countries, getting a stake in their resource development and extraction. Perhaps, more than any other country, China is making big steps to obtain direct access to fuel and mineral resources in Africa, Latin America, and Asia.

The United States and European countries are supplied a signifi-cant portion of the natural resources they consume by major multina-tional companies such as Exxon-Mobil, Royal-Dutch Shell, Rio-Tinto, or BHP Billiton. In Japan and South Korea, a key role is played by the resource supply channels of leading trading houses like Mitsubishi Corporation, Itochu, SK Corporation, or Hanwha Trading. State-owned resource companies play their part, too. In most other coun-tries, China included, supplies are provided first of all by state-owned oil and mining corporations.

Currently, with strong support from the state, China's natural resources heavyweights—PetroChina, Sinopec, CNOOC, Chinalco, China Metallurgical Group and the like—are establishing themselves among the leading global players, not at all inferior to Western majors or Japanese and Korean trading houses.

On its part, the Chinese government is coming out with an inno-vative model of tapping natural resources in Africa, Latin America, and Asia. In broader terms, this model helps China to strengthen its overall presence and influence in the Third World.

China is breaking existing rules in three major ways.

First, it combines participation in the resource development proj-ects in the Third World countries with large-scale development assis-tance focused on the building of their infrastructure. The government is acting in tandem with resource companies, providing financial and organizational support. Western firms do not work together with their governments in this fashion and thus cannot offer similar packages. (To compete with China, Japan and South Korea are starting to rapidly move in the same direction at this point.)

Second, the development assistance China provides is, mostly, neither official development aid (a developing country itself, China does not want to bear donors' responsibilities), nor purely commercial loans and investment. It is something in between: concessional loans (extended on better terms than commercial credit) and investment backed and subsidized by the state. China often extends resource-backed development loans, meaning that the borrower pays its debt not in cash but with oil, cocoa beans, or metal ores. It is a mutually beneficial scheme. The Chinese side gets resources it needs, while cash-stripped loan recipients do not have to pay in precious hard currency. In the late 1970s, to build its own infrastructure, China obtained similar loans from Japan leveraging its coal, oil, and other resources.

Third, unlike the West and to its great embarrassment, China's assistance is not conditioned on the recipient states' record regarding democratization, human rights, economic liberalization, or anticorruption measures. To access natural resources, it does not hesitate to cooperate with the most dictatorial and abusive regimes in the world. In such countries it easily becomes a de facto monopolist as Western firms are prohibited from going there by law.

Compared to the West, China provides its assistance quicker and more easily, without complicated screening procedures, and often on a larger scale.

African Saga

Let us pick up Africa as one of the major examples.

Here, between 2004 and 2010, Beijing concluded agreements on the resource-backed loans with at least seven states for a total of nearly $14 billion. It extended the oil-backed loan to Angola with Chinese companies building roads, railways, hospitals, schools, and water systems. Nigeria got two loans to finance projects for utilization of gas to generate electricity. The hydropower project in the Congo was prepaid in oil and the one in Ghana in cocoa beans. The former also received a $3 billion copper-backed loan to build infrastructure, hospitals, and universities.

In 2004, the Export-Import Bank of China extended three loans to the Angolan government at interest rates ranging from LIBOR plus 1.25 percent to LIBOR plus 1.75 percent, with generous grace periods and long repayment terms. Commercial lenders, such as Standard Chartered Bank, charged Angola LIBOR plus 2.5 percent or more, without any grace periods, and required faster repayment. China's $3 billion joint mining venture in the Congo gives the Congolese government a 32 percent stake, while in the joint ventures (JVs) with companies from other countries its share ranges from 7 percent to 25 percent (Brautigam 2010).

Also, China is starting to actively create and manage Special Trade and Economic Cooperation zones in Nigeria, Egypt, Ethiopia, Mauritius, Zambia, and so on, building infrastructure and facilities, especially with the aim of boosting low-cost manufacturing production and exports. This is exactly what African countries need to diversify and upgrade their industrial structure and to create jobs. In fact, the Chinese are replicating their own pattern of economic development at its earlier stages.

The zones also serve as platforms for the entry by Chinese companies searching for new markets and lower costs. Encouraging the transfer of production of low-end and/or energy-intensive manufacturing items, the government subsidizes part of their start-up expenses. The $5 billion China-Africa Development Fund has acquired equity shares in three of the seven planned zones (Brautigam 2010).

In contrast, the U.S. Congress does not allow the U.S. Agency of International Development to finance any activities leading to the relocation of Americans' jobs overseas.

He Acts While Other Men Just Talk

In November 2009, exactly when America and its allies were urging President Karzai of Afghanistan to be serious about fighting corruption in his regime, China Metallurgical Group Corp. made its entry into the country winning, for $800 million, a bid for the stake in the development of one of the world's largest copper ore deposits. According to the *Washington Post* and the Associated Press, citing informed sources in the U.S. military, to become a winner, the Chinese side paid a $30 million bribe to Afghanistan's minister of mines Muhammad Ibrahim Adel (Partlow 2009). The Minister denied the allegations.

The total amount of the Chinese investment into the deposit development will be almost $3 billion, the largest foreign investment in Afghanistan ever. As there is no railroad to transport the ore and the power plant to supply energy, China pledged to construct both (Taniguchi 2009).

China Has Become a Major Source of Development Aid

If concessional loans and government-backed subsidized investments are counted as development assistance, China has already become one of the major sources of aid for Africa, Latin America, and Asia, comparable to any major donor among the industrially developed states. As its assistance is highly concentrated on the development of natural resources and infrastructure, in these areas, for a non-negligible number of developing countries, especially in Africa, it is already number one.

According to the assessment by the researchers from New York University's Robert F. Wagner Graduate School of Public Service, the amount of China's development assistance increased from less than $1 billion in 2002 to $25 billion in 2007 (Lum et al. 2009). As of 2007, assistance was extended to 62 states. Africa received the greatest amount: $17,962 million. Latin America got just $401 million, but after $16,425 million in 2006. Southeast Asia's portion was $6,735 million. Out of the total, 66 percent was provided in the form of concessional loans or credit lines, 29 percent state-sponsored investment, and the remaining 5 percent as grants, debt cancellations, and in-kind aid.

For comparison, the U.S. foreign operations budget in 2008 (the total of bilateral development aid, economic security and military assistance, multilateral assistance, and food aid) was estimated at $24 billion.

Almost all China's assistance targets natural resources extraction and infrastructure/public works projects. In 2002–2007, allocations for natural resource extraction projects accounted for $9,432 million of assistance to Africa, $18,525 million for Latin America, and $4,788 million for Southeast Asia. The scale of financing of infrastructure/public works projects reached $17,865 million, $7,535 million, and $6,438 million respectively. Aid is highly concentrated on resource-rich countries like

Angola, the Congo, Sudan, Mozambique, Equatorial Guinea, Nigeria, Ethiopia, and Gabon (Lum et al. 2009). On the other hand, the scale of humanitarian aid, as well as technical and military assistance is minor.

Within less than one decade, China has established direct access to a wide range of natural resources in the developing countries. Through active resource diplomacy, it has also dramatically raised its overall economic and political clout in the Third World. For many developing nations all around the globe, it has rapidly grown into the most or one of the most important economic partners. The West becomes increasingly nervous about Beijing's rising influence and warns developing states of the dangers of China's tight embrace.

Chapter 18

Indigenous Innovation: Seeking to Command Advanced Technologies by All Means

C
hina is rushing to access the world's most advanced technologies and to become a leader in research and development. The
China-West technology war has begun.

About 10 years ago, at a Russo-Japanese gathering of leading
experts on international affairs, during a debate on China and its new
global role, a prominent Russian scholar (expressing his personal point
of view) bluntly told the Japanese side: "It was you who created this
economic and political monster. Now we all have to pay the price."
He meant massive Japanese (and generally Western) investment in
China and a large-scale official development aid as major prerequisites
for its spurt and emergence as a superpower.

The formula is largely correct if you accept the wording. Let us put it this way: Western investment and development aid contributed a lot to the birth of a new superpower of a size and character never seen before, which is now posing unprecedented challenges for the West itself. As far as the economic dimension is concerned, until recently the formula applied to production and exports.

The West Is Creating China as a New Technological Superpower

Why did the West do it? Obviously, because with its gigantic pool of cheap and efficient labor and the world's most dynamic market, China provided unique business opportunities. Due to this uniqueness, it faced no big problems with using Western capital, technologies, and expertise to become the world's largest manufacturer and exporter of a wide range of low-end products.

Nowadays, China is interested in foreign capital for a different reason. As far as low-end manufacturing is concerned, it has accumulated more than enough capital, technologies, and expertise to do it all by itself. For Western businesses, it may still be attractive to move to China to produce something simple and cheap. However, this is not the major thing today's China wants them to do. Furthermore, it often does not want them to do it at all. Not surprisingly, the Chinese government did not think twice before abruptly eliminating across-the-board tax privileges for foreign-owned firms in 2007. Sometimes it does not even stop short of blocking a foreign investment project altogether when it targets a low-end and, especially, environment-unfriendly manufacturing.

Nowadays China does not need just money. It needs advanced technologies to upgrade its industries and wants Western companies to bring them in. And for this purpose it leverages its unique labor pool and market expansion dynamics in exactly the same way it leveraged them in the past to encourage foreign investment in low-end manufacturing.

And this time, too, Western companies are doing what China wants them to do: They are becoming important contributors to its technological upgrading. The formula cited at the beginning of this chapter applies again. Today it is largely the West itself that is creating China as a new technological superpower.

Soaring Foreign Investment in R&D Centers and Production Upgrading

As of late 2009, the number of independent R&D centers and in-house R&D departments established by foreign firms in China reached about 1,200 including the centers opened by over 400 firms on the list of Fortune 500 companies worldwide. Total registered capital of around 460 R&D centers approved by the Ministry of Commerce or local governments was $7.4 billion, and the total outstanding balance of investment into those centers hit $12.8 billion.

As of 2006, foreign firms accounted for 21 percent of all China-based R&D centers in large and medium-sized manufacturing and 19 percent of the entire R&D workforce. Their share of the total R&D expenditure in large and medium-sized manufacturing increased from 19.7 percent in 2002 to 27.2 percent in 2008. In 2008, they held 29 percent of all invention patents in the country (Jin 2010).

Foreign companies' research centers are concentrated in such fields as electronics (including software), telecommunications, biotechnology and pharmaceuticals, chemicals, and automobiles. Leading global firms (Microsoft, IBM, Motorola, Intel, GE, 3M, Sun Microsystems, Pfizer, Siemens, Philips, Volkswagen, and Fujitsu to name just a few) started to establish themselves, with high frequency from the late 1990s to the early 2000s. As time goes by, the pace is accelerating. In recent years, France Telecom and Docomo have opened R&D centers in 3G mobile communications; GM, Nissan, and Hyundai in the auto industry; Roche, Novartis, Sanofi-Aventis, AstraZeneca, and Merck Serono in pharmaceuticals; Dow, Exxon Mobile, and Bayer in chemicals, and so on.

More and more often, China-based centers are transformed into or initially created as centers on the regional or global scale.

For instance, in 2009 Novartis announced that within five years it would expand its Shanghai R&D facility into a global center and invest an additional $1 billion. Microsoft established Microsoft Research China in Beijing in 1998, upgraded it to Microsoft Research Asia in

2001, and then opened The Science and Technology Park in Shanghai in 2010 as its global research center outside the United States. Sanofi-Aventis transformed its China R&D Center in Shanghai to the Asia-Pacific Research Center, covering also Japan, Russia, and India. Having invested 100 million euros, Bayer&Schering Pharma launched its R&D Center in Beijing in February 2009, giving it the status of the global center from the very start (Jin 2010).

Going beyond product development for the Chinese market, foreign companies' centers are increasingly engaged in basic research. With a certain time lag, R&D activities are globalizing in the same way as production. Global companies are doing their research on a global basis, choosing venues providing high-qualified human resource and attractive in terms of cost, infrastructure, and legal and regulatory environment. In spite of its notoriously lax intellectual property rules, China has managed to position itself as one of the most attractive R&D platforms in the world—most of all because of its widening pool of capable researchers who are still cheap by international standards. On its part, the Chinese government exempts taxes on R&D centers' equipment imports and provides R&D subsidies.

Products manufactured by foreign companies at their Chinese factories are also significantly upgraded. More and more often, they go far beyond simple labor-intensive manufacturing, choosing to combine advanced technologies with the cost advantages China provides. It applies to both final and intermediate products, giving multinationals new important benefits. For instance, manufacturers of cars or electronic devices transferring production of parts or materials to China get much greater cost advantages than those who transfer assembly operations only.

A close look at the new investment projects launched by foreign firms in China nowadays clearly shows that many of them are related to production upgrading, the transfer of advanced technologies, or to the creation of R&D facilities.

Mitsubishi Chemical and Mitsubishi Plastic Engineering established a joint venture with Sinopec to make high-end resins used in the manufacturing of auto and electronic parts, optical disks, and construction materials. LG Electronics has started producing advanced models of LCD TVs. Siemens has built a plant to manufacture parts for wind energy generating equipment, and Daikin will make key parts for inverter-type air-conditioners in a joint venture with Gree Electric Appliances. Honda will start local production of electric vehicles. In Shanghai, FIAT has established an R&D facility to develop engine-manufacturing technologies, Britain's Astra Zeneca to conduct research on new anticancer drugs, and Panasonic to develop home electronic appliances tailored to the needs of Chinese consumers. Exxon Mobile Chemical has announced the start of applied research and development of chemical products. The list can be continued.

China's Technological Strategy

China is no longer just a global factory producing low-cost simple goods. It is also establishing its position as a global center of high-tech manufacturing and a global research lab, opening unique opportunities to combine advanced technologies and high quality of products with competitive costs.

The transfer of advanced foreign technologies to China is intensifying by itself, driven by the hand of the global market.

However, the Chinese government wants to speed up the process and, most of all, to raise the innovative capability of Chinese domestic institutions and companies. This is the major motive behind the policy of the so-called indigenous innovation launched in 2006 which is causing a lot of controversy today. It was articulated in The National Medium and Long-Term Plan for the Development of Science and Technology for 2006–2020. Officially this policy has been elevated to the same strategic level as the openness and reform policy launched under Deng Xiaoping in the late 1970s and early 1980s.

The task is to turn China into a big technological power by 2020 and a global technology leader by 2050. The gross R&D expenditure has to be increased from 1.3 percent to 2.5 percent of GDP.

The plan designates eight key technological fields where 27 breakthrough technologies have to be pursued: biotechnology, IT, advanced materials, advanced manufacturing, advanced energy technology, marine technology, laser technology, and aerospace technology. The four major basic research programs are in protein science, nanotechnology, quantum physics, and developmental and reproductive science. The core of the plan is 16 megaprojects supported by massive government financing, in such areas as core electronic components, high-end chips, and basic software products; large-scale integrated circuits manufacturing equipment; advanced NC machinery; advanced nuclear reactors; breeding new varieties of genetically modified organisms; pharmaceutical innovation and development; and so on. The plan sets the goal of reducing overall reliance on foreign technologies to 30 percent from an estimated 60 percent in 2006 (U.S. Chamber of Commerce 2010).

Technology Transfer Enforcement

The indigenous innovation policy is officially defined as the one "enhancing original innovation through co-innovation and re-innovation based on the assimilation of the imported technologies" (U.S. Chamber of Commerce 2010).

The idea itself, by and large, looks quite relevant. If you want to become an innovator yourself, developing original technologies and products, you should first of all learn what has been achieved by your predecessors, and it would be logical to start with innovating together with them or adding new elements or features to their inventions. It helps to accumulate knowledge and develop skills necessary to proceed to your own original research and development. This is the way it was done by Japan, South Korea, Taiwan, and others who followed America and Europe on the innovation path.

The problem, however, is that China seeks to achieve this basically relevant goal using a Chinese cocktail of policies that create unequal conditions for competition between domestic and foreign firms, effectively help the former to steal overseas technologies and designs, and force foreign companies to share technologies against their will.

The Patent Law makes it possible for Chinese firms to obtain junk patents issued quickly and without in-depth examination. They serve as a tool to retaliate against overseas intellectual property rights (IPR) lawsuits. Testing and approval procedures for imported products have been deliberately made complicated and time-consuming in order to erect import barriers on the one hand and to learn foreign designs and production processes on the other.

The Anti-Monopoly Law can be used against foreign companies refusing to disclose their technologies and know-how. For instance, the list of the "abuses" of the law by MNCs included Cisco's refusal to license its Internet protocol (IP) to Chinese companies that wanted to connect to its network equipment (U.S. Chamber of Commerce 2010).

The most controversial component of the indigenous innovation policy is China's government procurement system. According to the Government Procurement Law adopted in 2002, purchases by government organizations, with a few exceptions, have to be limited to domestically made products. In May 2007, "Measures for Administration of Government Procurement Budgets for Indigenous Innovation Products" prescribed governments at all levels to compile indigenous innovation procurement plans. In December of the same year, the Ministry of Finance issued "Measures for the Administration of Government Procurement of Imported Products." To purchase imported goods, government entities were obliged to get an approval from a board of experts. Among foreign suppliers, they were recommended to favor those who transfer technologies and train Chinese personnel.

Next, in November 2009, the "Circular on Carrying Out the Work on Accreditation of National Indigenous Innovation Products" announced the creation of a new national level catalog of high-tech indigenous innovation products (in the areas of computers and communication, office equipment, software, energy devices, and so on) that were eligible for preferential treatment in government procurement. An indigenous innovation product was defined as the one that has IPR owned by a Chinese company and a commercial trademark initially registered inside China.

A month later the government produced a catalog of 240 types of equipment whose production by domestic companies would be encouraged in order to upgrade the country's manufacturing base. Along with a priority status as indigenous innovation products suppliers, their makers were promised tax incentives and R&D subsidies.

Western governments and businesses strongly urged Beijing to readjust the government procurement system as it effectively deprived foreign companies of the access to this very substantial segment of the Chinese market.

In April 2010, the Circular was reversed. The requirements about the IPR ownership by a Chinese company and initial registration of the trademark in China were dropped.

Also, the Chinese side proclaimed that preferential treatment of and incentives for producers of indigenous innovation products were fully applicable to foreign-owned companies operating in China. The government procurement system was modified to prioritize domestically designed and manufactured goods (meaning that the value created inside China exceeds a certain percentage of the total value—normally 50 percent) including those designed and manufactured by foreign-invested firms.

From the very start of the market reforms, China's message to foreign companies has been "Better produce in China than export to China." This time it added a new message of a similar character: "Better innovate in China (and share your technologies) than in your home country or anywhere else." It looked almost like an ultimatum: Unless you innovate and produce inside China you won't be allowed to sell to the government.

The West protested.

In January 2011, President Hu Jintao promised President Obama to cancel the rule requiring foreign companies to design and manufacture inside the country the products they wanted to sell to Chinese government entities. In May the same year, at the U.S.-China Strategic and Economic Dialogue it was reportedly confirmed that the Chinese government would not buy indigenous innovation products on a preferential basis.

However, at the time of writing Western businessmen working in China are still complaining that procurement practices have not changed and provincial authorities appear or pretend to have heard nothing about the promises made by the central government. Is it just a familiar bureaucratic muddle and incoherence or a new way of pursuing the old policy? At this point it is still too early to give an accurate answer.

However, there is little doubt that China will continue to press foreign companies hard not only to bring in advanced technologies and products, but also, more and more, to develop them within its borders—even though they are already doing it at a rapidly growing scale on their own initiative.

Chapter 19

Company Acquisitions: Chinese Are More Active than Westerners

One more area of high China-West tensions is company acquisitions. While Chinese companies, including state-owned enterprises (SOEs), are moving to acquire Western firms on an increasingly large scale, acquisitions of Chinese companies by their Western counterparts remain modest in terms of both the number of transactions and their value.

In 2010, the total value of cross-border M&A transactions (announced deals) involving Chinese firms reached $80.7 billion, as opposed to $63.6 billion in 2009. The total value of deals involving European firms was $641 billion, and firms from the Americas $1.13 trillion (Simpson Thatcher & Barlett 2011).

Acquisitions Asymmetry

Chinese companies are mostly playing the role of acquirers, not the acquired. For instance, in the mining industry China accounted for $17 billion, or 22 percent of all cross-border M&A in the world in 2009. A review by Deloitte shows that only between early 2009 and mid-2010, Chinese auto companies conducted 11 acquisitions abroad and their total value was $2.5 billion, while in 2005–2008 there were 12 acquisitions worth $1.3 billion (An 2011).

In contrast, in China itself, M&A accounted for only about 3 percent of the total amount of inward foreign direct investment (FDI) in 2010, while the global figure was 70 percent (*China Post* 2011). Three percent of the total means just a little more than $3 billion.

Chinese acquisitions of large Western companies or their departments have become a hot topic of the day. Perhaps you won't think twice before giving such widely known examples as the purchase of IBM's PC department by Lenovo and of Volvo by Geely. Geely also bought Australia's Drivetrain, one of the world's leading suppliers of automotive transmissions. If you try to recollect more, probably, you will name the acquisitions of Ogihara's mold models production factory by BYD (Ogihara is one of the largest mold models producers in Japan), of Quorum Systems, a radio equipment maker from San Diego, by semiconductors manufacturer Spreadtrum Communications, or of the Dutch producer of specialized transportation equipment Burg Industries by China's International Marine Containers Group.

On the other hand, you won't find equally famous and impressive examples of large-scale acquisitions of Chinese companies by Western firms, though, of course, they are not at a zero level. For instance, L'Oreal acquired cosmetic brand Yue-Sai, which belonged to Coty Inc., and made a successful bid for Shenzhen-based Raystar Cosmetics, one of China's top three skincare brands. The U.S. restaurant operator Yum! Brands (the owner of Pizza Hut, KFC, and Taco Bell) is moving to acquire hot-pot restaurant chain Little Sheep. Home Depot bought local home-improvement chain Home Way.

Where does this asymmetry come from?

The Chinese Government
Is Tightening Regulations

One of the major reasons is the Chinese government's rather negative attitude toward foreign acquisitions of important domestic companies.

Existing regulations make an acquisition of any important Chinese company by foreigners extremely difficult and often effectively impossible (though the government is calling on foreign investors to participate in the reorganization of domestic enterprises through equity investment and M&A, especially in high-end manufacturing and energy/environment-related areas, and endorses acquisitions matching its policies). China is channeling the inward FDI toward, first, joint ventures with domestic companies, second, greenfield investment, and third, acquisitions of minority stakes—especially in case an important state-owned/state-holding company is involved.

The regulation introduced back in 2006, allegedly in reaction to the blocking by the U.S. Congress of the acquisition of American oil company Unocal by one of China's petroleum giants CNOOC, gives the Ministry of Commerce (MOC) the right to examine and declare void any acquisition if, in its opinion, it can adversely affect national security and important industries or if it targets a domestic company possessing a famous or historical brand. Also, if the acquirer is of a certain size and has a sufficient market in China (the size and market are not specified—very Chinese-style), any acquisition has to get an approval from the MOC and the State Administration of Industry and Commerce (SAIC).

Notably, in 2009 the Chinese government disallowed Coca-Cola's acquisition of China Huiyuan Juice Group, which would have been the largest in the country's history. The U.S. private equity fund Carlyle Group had to backtrack on its plan to acquire an 85 percent stake in Xudong Construction, accepting 45 percent while the majority stake went to Xuzhou Machinery Group owned by the Xuzhou city government (Chung 2007).

In February 2011, China announced a plan to establish a ministerial panel to review foreign takeovers of domestic companies. It is to be led by the National Development and Reform Commission and MOC, and overseen by the State Council. Its task is to scrutinize acquisitions involving military industrial companies and other defense-related firms, but also companies in agriculture, energy, and natural resources, and some parts of infrastructure and transportation services. It is said to be modeled after a similar institution in the United States and created with the aim of increasing the transparency of procedures.

Western Governments Are Blocking Chinese Acquisitions of Technology and Resource Firms

For its part, the West is also cautious about Chinese acquisitions of its firms, but overall the restrictions it imposes are less tight than those that Western acquirers are facing in China.

Take a close look at the Chinese attempts to acquire Western companies, and you will see that they can be divided mainly into three big groups. First, the Chinese buy ailing but famous firms striving to keep afloat, or firms that, like IBM, are interested in selling out an interest in a less technologically advanced sector to climb further up the value chain. They purchase their brands and obtain technologies, know-how, distribution networks, and high-skilled personnel. Second, they are interested in buying dynamic technology companies, including small and medium entities. Third, they are targeting natural resource firms.

Acquisitions of resources and high technology companies face a lot of obstacles on their way and often fail, especially when the targeted Western firm is a big and important player. The West reciprocates, not letting China obtain control over its key resources and technologies.

In 2009, an Anglo-Australian mining giant Rio-Tinto withdrew from a deal to sell substantial stakes to Chinalco. A telecom equipment maker Huawei was barred from purchasing America's 3Com in 2008 and then mobile wireless network division of Motorola and an Internet broadband software company 2Wire in 2010. The major reason was the Western side's concerns about national security risks posed by China's control over crucially important natural resources and industries—especially because Chinalco is a state-owned company and Huawei is reported to have close ties to the Chinese government and the military.

However, Chinese acquisitions of the first type—ailing companies with famous brands—proceed rather smoothly. In the West, they don't meet much resistance and are even encouraged in order to support business activities and preserve employment.

This inevitably leads to the acquisitions asymmetry because similar acquisitions of Chinese firms by Westerners are not on track.

Chinese Acquirers Are Backed by the State

Finally, there is one more factor, or rather two closely interrelated factors of the acquisition asymmetry, which also comprise the major reason for the China-West acquisitions wars. First, like no other country in the world, China has positioned its state-owned companies as major cross-border acquirers. Second, most of the major Chinese acquisitions (even by non-state-owned firms) are feared to be state-backed.

In the end it often turns out that, in fact, it is the Chinese state that is acquiring Western private companies one after another, albeit indirectly. On the contrary, almost all Western acquirers are purely private firms.

As a rule, Chinese acquirers get the foreign currency they need to carry out the transaction not through the foreign exchange market but in a nontransparent way, directly from a state-owned bank—eventually from the state. If the Chinese government considers a particular transaction strategically important to access mineral resources, technologies, and brands, or to boost its geopolitical clout in general, it can allocate much greater funds than those affordable for a private company sticking to the market rationale.

Again, China drastically changes the rules of the game in the global business arena. To tackle this structural asymmetry, the West has no choice but to put every Chinese acquisition under scrutiny.

On the other hand, at this point not only Chinese, but Western governments have not clearly articulated their basic policy concept on the acquisitions pursued by foreign state-owned or government-linked companies. As long as it is not done, their responses will remain spontaneous.

Conclusion

The West Needs a Cohesive China Policy and Unconventional Responses to China-Posed Challenges

We have outlined five major areas where China and the West are in an economic war.

In all of them China is mostly on the offensive. It appears that more often than not it is effectively setting the terms of the game, or rather the battle, while the frustrated West expresses its dissatisfaction and dismay, but mostly fails to prevent it.

In spite of all the objections from its Western counterparts, China continues to appreciate yuan at the slow pace it prefers.

It is aggressively expanding its trade surplus and continues to rely on exporting industries as major growth drivers. Its rapidly expanding market is captured more by domestic companies than Western exporters. Its currency, trade, and industrial policies induce Western firms not to export, but to produce locally.

Beijing has bluntly rejected the framework proposed by the West on the CO_2 emissions cuts. Having refused to take binding obligations, it is pressing Western states to support its (and other developing countries') voluntary steps in this area, in addition to making cuts of their own, which will be, of course, mandatory.

More and more, China is obtaining direct access to natural resources around the Third World, boosting its overall economic and political clout in Asia, Africa, and Latin America. Its national oil and other resource companies are rapidly expanding their global presence, challenging Western competitors, leading multinationals included.

China is emerging as a new world center of technological innovation and one of the major R&D platforms. At the same time it is successfully fostering the transfer of advanced Western technologies, often making it a condition for accessing its domestic market or doing business on its territory. Many new foreign direct investment projects in the country are related to production upgrading and R&D.

Finally, supported by the state, Chinese companies have quickly joined the ranks of the world's leading international acquirers targeting and purchasing a wide range of Western firms, while the West's acquisitions record in China is more modest.

Leveraging its new economic and financial strength, China has developed a remarkably strong bargaining power, or, in broader terms, a power to make things on the global economic arena the way it wants them to be. For the West, it is often difficult to find an antidote.

For example, imposing high punitive tariffs does not help to protect domestic industries and may backfire in various ways. Threatening to label China as a currency manipulator, with all the dire consequences this may bring, does not look like a well-founded and productive bargaining strategy, either.

Policies that worked against the West's earlier challengers are not applicable. It doesn't make sense to try to exhaust China economically in an arms race as happened to the former Soviet Union. There are no close political and defense relationships that can be leveraged to win concessions on the economic front like the ones that existed with Japan when it posed its great economic challenge in the 1970s and 1980s. It is also very difficult to resolve problems between the West and Beijing by applying the rules set by international institutions like WTO—they appear to be incomplete, ambiguous, or difficult to enforce.

Perhaps the West still has not developed techniques and methods workable enough to leverage its own strong points.

China is getting economically stronger against the West for two major reasons. First, it has much greater potential to grow, stemming from larger increments in inputs of capital and labor, more rapidly elevating productivity, and effectively, much faster increase of all the components of final demand. Remaining highly competitive in terms of cost, it rapidly climbs up the value chain, conquering high-tech segments of the global market. Moreover, compared to most Western economies, it appears to be stronger macroeconomically and structurally. This is a real thing. And, in order not to lose, the West simply has to make its economies more competitive: first of all, to accelerate the rise of their *quality* in the broadest meaning of the word, which includes productivity, technological sophistication, quality of products and services, product differentiation, and branding. Also, it has to double and triple its effort to overcome existing structural biases (see Part Two) and put its fiscal house in order. To use a soccer analogy, the Western team has to become stronger physically, technically, and tactically.

The second reason for the dramatic growth of China's economic clout is not a real thing. Chinese chemistry is at work. The soccer game between China and the West is played on the ground whose surface is inclined toward the West's goal. Instead of a level playing field, China-West economic relations contain many asymmetries. Using a variety of pretexts and tools, the Chinese side aptly creates conditions favorable for itself and unfavorable for its competitors. Its currency is undervalued. Chinese companies rely on a heavy state support including injections of public funds. Complete acquisitions of important domestic firms by Western counterparts are effectively impossible, while the list of Chinese acquisitions in the West is already quite long. Western firms' access to important segments of the Chinese market and sometimes even the opportunity to do business in China as such are linked to technology transfers, while China's legal framework and current policies leave big loopholes for technology theft. And so on.

In this situation, Western countries currently don't seem to have a cohesive policy to address China-posed challenges. That's why, more often than not, the ball is rolling along the tilted playground closer and closer to the West's goal.

Logically, the viable solution for the West is to substantially level the playing field (complete leveling is hardly possible as China remains a developing country), eliminating or at least reducing existing asymmetries. The time is ripe to make *symmetry*, or equality of conditions, a key word.

Two things have to be made clear in this regard. First, challenges posed by such an unconventional counterpart as China can hardly be addressed only by conventional means. Second, a set of retaliation tools and policies has to be in place to contain China's moves to tilt the playground toward the West's goal.

What can be done?

First, the policy of promoting exports to China has to be significantly amplified. It is vital to pursue it more actively and on a permanent basis, covering a wide range of domestic companies, both large and small. A drastic increase of China-bound exports, not a trade deficit reduction through containing the imports of made-in-China goods, should be fixed as a priority policy goal. A clear message to the Chinese side has to be sent about the urgency of this task.

It is important to emphasize as strongly as possible that, at the present stage of China's economic development, more exports of Western goods are indispensable to raise the living standards of its citizens. (When in China, you feel this almost physically if you find time for a tour around local retail outlets.) In other words, the Chinese government's stance on the import issue can be presented as a test of its willingness to make the life of the Chinese people better.

In the early 1980s, then Japanese Prime Minister Yasuhiro Nakasone bought an imported shirt in front of the TV and photo cameras, and the inscription on the baggage carts at the Narita Airport said, IMPORT NOW. America and the West in general did not spare their efforts to persuade Japan that growing imports are needed for its own sake and for the benefit of Japanese consumers. And this strategy made sense. Frankly, questions about the openness of the Japanese market and availability of a relevant range of imported consumer goods at reasonable prices remain even at this point. However, without any doubt, today here in Japan we have many more West-made products than in Prime Minister Nakasone's times, and it does make the life of Japanese families better. Perhaps the time is ripe to unleash similar policies with regard to China, though, of course, their methods will have to be different (it is difficult to imagine the Chinese PM buying an imported shirt to encourage the purchases of overseas products or IMPORT NOW carts in the Beijing or Shanghai airport).

As mentioned in Part One, Western governments, both central and local, can do much more to help domestic producers find their way to Chinese consumers. This effort involves promotion of products, establishment of efficient distribution channels, and removal of various kinds of systemic, bureaucratic, and lack-of-information impediments. Currently, many producers in America and Europe, potentially able of exporting to China, are simply unaware of existing opportunities and don't have an idea where they can get information about them. They do not go out to actively search for such information both because they are busy and because they don't believe that such a strategy can work. Governments must show them the way.

Next, though proclaiming Beijing a currency manipulator and imposing punitive import tariffs is, in our view, meaningless. Western firms exporting to China, logically, have the right to claim an export subsidy to make up for losses caused by the undervalued yuan.

When exporting to China, Western companies are directly competing with domestic producers in the segment of differentiated products—in *their* segment, where they do have a rationale to produce and need fair price competition to position themselves in the Chinese market. Currently the Barbie doll is outsold in China by the local Kurhn brand, largely because the latter is cheaper. If the yuan exchange rate were higher, Barbie's yuan-based price would fall, and it would sell better. For example, if the yuan is undervalued by 40 percent, there is a rationale for subsidizing (in fact, countersubsidizing) Western exporters the dollar, euro, or whatever equivalent of 40 yuan for every product they have to sell at 100 yuan at the current exchange rate—so that they could sell it for 60 yuan and expand their customer base. And this would be absolutely fair.

In reality it is hardly possible on such a scale—both because of the West's financial constraints (also, again, don't forget that China is its major creditor), and because it may mean the start of an all-out trade war.

Yet, within feasible limits, it would be more than relevant to consider various financial support scenarios for those business heroes who face the challenge to export to China in spite of the present exchange rates disparity. For example, central or local governments might bear the burden of market research and sale promotion costs. Exporters to China could get some kind of a tax refund—the way Chinese exporters do—or preferential loans from state financial institutions. Such measures could be applied to exports to other countries with controlled and undervalued currencies as well.

Second, environmental issues have to be placed more in the center of the China-West economic relationship. The West eventually has no choice but to make a concession accepting that China (and other major developing countries) will target CO_2 cuts per unit of the GDP, not in absolute terms. However, at the same time America and Europe should attach much higher priority to bilateral environmental projects, making sure that China pays in full for the equipment, technologies, and solutions it acquires within their framework, and continuing to press for preferential treatment of environmental products and services it imports. This is fair play.

Third, in today's world, with China-imposed very tough and largely unconventional rules of competition, the West does not have to be shy about strong government leadership in order to promote further economic upgrading to enhance global competitiveness. Among other things, it concerns such areas as the creation and expansion of key new industries, like renewable energy or production of electric vehicles, and the fight for the share of the global infrastructure market. Western countries have to learn the art of competing with China not only at the company-to-company level, but also at the government-to-government level. "Left alone" and having to stand against Chinese competitors acting in tandem with their state, Western firms (even leading multinationals) will be on the losing side.

This does not mean that Western governments should invest in new industries directly as much as the Chinese government does, or that the primary role of the private sector has to be reconsidered.

However, an increase of the targeted state support for key frontier sectors is an urgent task. Assistance in market creation for domestic producers and strong financial incentives for buyers of innovative products should be among the major priorities. Western governments have to double and triple their efforts to foster the formation of strong industrial clusters, promote closer links between companies and research institutions, drastically improve education and training systems, and upgrade infrastructure.

Fourth, the West should be more active in counterbalancing China's growing influence in the Third World and its global rush for natural resources. There is nothing wrong in any Western state initiating package deals with resource-rich developing countries, combining resource extraction and supply arrangements with assistance in the infrastructure development, as well as capacity building and other areas. To launch projects of this kind, Western governments can work together with their domestic resource firms somewhat in the Chinese way, even if those firms are major multinationals. It is important to think about additional rewards for developing countries having a better record on democratization, human rights, antigraft policies, and economic reforms.

Fifth, the West has to be ready to retaliate against China's indigenous innovation policy when it creates unequal conditions for competition, violates intellectual property rights (IPRs) and, especially, restricts the market access.

For example, it has every reason to clearly articulate the policy of denying access of Western markets to Chinese companies found responsible for IPR abuses, provided there is evidence based on thorough investigation. The results of such investigations should be made public and explained in detail to the Chinese side.

As long as the issue of preferential treatment of indigenous innovation products by the Chinese government has not been settled, it is logical to attach symmetrical conditions for Chinese firms seeking to sell to Western government agencies, state-owned companies, and public entities. A more radical option would be to close the government procurement market for Chinese state-owned enterprises (SOEs) altogether.

Sixth, full symmetry has to be provided regarding company acquisitions. As long as important, especially state-owned, companies in China effectively cannot be acquired by Western firms, full acquisitions of important Western firms by Chinese state-owned and state-holding companies also have to be basically banned, and those by nonstate companies severely restricted. Exceptions are relevant only when a Chinese acquisition is considered beneficial for a recipient country due to its contribution to the revitalization of a domestic industry or region and job creation. An acquisition of an important Western company by any Chinese firm should require approval procedures similar, at least in terms of thoroughness and complexity, to those that Western acquirers have to go through in China. This is necessary to encourage Chinese authorities to be more efficient and constructive. Symmetric conditions may be set regarding the share of domestic capital in particular industries. Guiding Chinese acquirers to choose a joint venture or a minority stake purchase option could also be a good idea.

Today's China is a unique superpower, posing unique challenges. To address them, the West has to come up with a well-founded and comprehensive China policy, going beyond the range of conventional tools and concepts. This policy has to be creative and flexible, but firm. It should combine strategies to promote partnership and productive interactions with a persistent effort to provide a level playing field.

Otherwise the economic wars with China will be lost. The stakes are high.

Epilogue

China, the West, and the World

We have examined the three major dimensions of the West-to-China economic power shift.

First, China is rapidly elevating its role as the world's leader in manufacturing production and merchandise exports. As far as the might of the state is concerned, it has also emerged as a leading financial power. It is becoming an increasingly important player in high-tech industries and R&D. Its service industries are growing fast as well, but in this area the West retains a noticeable lead.

Second, in the wake of the global—or rather Western—crisis of 2008–2009 and in its aftermath, the Chinese economy has proved to be structurally stronger than most economies in the West. It is resilient to the structural diseases the West failed to prevent several years ago. China's macroeconomic condition is also much better. The Chinese model of state-private capitalism has displayed its strong points.

Third, in almost all the major areas where economic interests of China and the West clash, China is showing a remarkable ability to make things go in the direction it wants them to. This is often achieved by imposing unequal conditions of competition: The playground where the China-West competition game is played is often inclined toward the West's goal.

China is changing history, economic history included. The largest country on earth with the most rapidly growing economy and dramatically increasing global clout has established a unique position in the world.

Where does China's uniqueness come from? We define the following five features.

The first one is the combination of the market economy and complete non-Westernness.

Today's China is the first major power in modern history that has a market, or *capitalist*, economy, but does not belong to the Western world, is not engaged to it through any economic, political or military alliance, and is not strongly influenced by its institutions, values, and culture. The former Soviet Union did not have a market economy and did not compete in the global markets of the vast majority of goods and services. Postwar Japan developed a very close political and defense relationship with the West, first of all the United States, created a similar political system, and, as time went by, increasingly absorbed Western-style market economy concepts, along with Western culture and values in general. India has historically close ties with the West in many areas and worships Western-style democracy.

China is pragmatic, but absolutely non-Western. Therefore, though in the process of the structural transformation of its economy it may actively accommodate many elements of the Western capitalist system, it is not at all inclined to share basic Western concepts about the rules and principles the market economy has to adhere to.

Second, the non-Westernness of China's economic system stems most of all from the role of the state, which is greater and wider than in any Western nation.

The Chinese state is not bound by the conceptual constraints imposed by Western pro-market ideologies and does not hesitate to throw its weight behind domestic companies to help them strengthen their global position. At the same time, it not only supports industries and enterprises, but also plays the role of a demanding, effectively capitalist owner keeping managers on the run to enhance the companies' efficiency and, yes, also investors' returns. Quite often, it willingly invites the private sector to co-invest.

Third, China is unique in terms of not only economic growth rates, but also the length of its high growth period. It has not experienced a recession or even a significant slowdown all through the decades of market reforms unveiled in the late 1970s. Conventional economic wisdom says, "Never assume that growth will never end." The market economy is unthinkable without busts. The day, or rather the year will come when China's growth will fall to a very low level or even become negative. However, it will happen only in a distant future.

Growth cannot be eternal. Yet, it is time to recognize and clearly say that China has discovered an "algorithm" for maintaining rapid growth for an exceptionally long period of time, suppressing all downward pressures coming from cyclical fluctuations, external shocks or whatever. This algorithm is a combination of several major components. Their list starts with the Chinese economy's outstanding ability to preserve, within a long period of time, a rapid investment expansion. The second component is a continuous steady rise of labor inputs in the industrial and service sectors, especially due to a very large-scale migration from rural areas. The third one is a long wave of the growth of domestic demand as hundreds and hundreds of millions of Chinese are rising from the strata of have-nots to the strata of haves. The domestic "flying geese" phenomenon is also very important: More advanced eastern coastal provinces are passing the growth relay baton to vast inland areas in the center, the west, and the northeast. Finally, the state is persistently shielding the growing national economy from a variety of financial risks (the ones that the West failed to contain several years ago), vigorously fighting overlending, overborrowing, and asset bubbles, tightly regulating transactions with high-risk financial instruments, strictly supervising banks, and so on.

Fourth, in today's global economy China has established a de facto monopolistic position as the major global platform for low-cost manufacturing (meaning that in this capacity it cannot be replaced by any other country), both low-tech and high-tech, and is now starting to emerge as a leading platform for low-cost research and development. Therefore, for a wide range of Western companies it has become a nonsubstitutable place to do business (which, of course, does not mean that there are no Western firms closing in China and moving somewhere else or choosing another country from the very start). On the contrary, China itself can substitute for any Western partner, even the United States, for another one, both as a source of inward investment and as a target for outbound investment by domestic firms.

The fifth unique feature is China money. Let the People Bank's governor say that $3 trillion plus foreign reserves is too much and difficult to manage. For technocrats it is definitely so. However, for the Chinese state, namely China's ruling elite, large assets provide both wealth and unprecedented leverage over those who are liable. It is very simple: One cannot talk hard to his banker. Soaring foreign reserves have turned Beijing into the West's major creditor, giving it enormous power to push its own interests whoever the counterpart is.

The China-versus-the-West economic relationship is also historically unique.

In the global capitalist economy, China has emerged as the first ever non-Western center of power (as mentioned, in this book we assume that Japan is also the West) whose size and economic might is comparable to that of the United States and effectively exceed those of any other developed country.

The China-West economic power shift marks the end of the era of a unipolar global capitalist economy with the U.S.-led developed West at its core. Today's global economy has already adopted a bipolar configuration, with the Chinese pole continuing to grow at a much greater speed than the Western one. It is becoming increasingly multipolar as other large emerging countries, one by one, are joining the ranks of fast runners. At this point, however, among the emerging market economies, only China has reached the scale and power making it a full-fledged competitor of the developed West. Indian, Brazilian, Russian and other major emerging economies are smaller in size and have established a noticeable global presence only in a significantly narrower range of industries.

Our analysis shows that the scope of manufacturing products, whose number one producer is China, has been drastically widening. The

Chinese lead in terms of production volumes has become a rule, and the sectors where it is not leading are more and more an exception.

The upgrading of China's manufacturing industry is gaining strength. The country is becoming an increasingly important producer of intermediate goods and various kinds of equipment. Chinese manufacturers feel more and more confident in the high-tech products segment and, in the domestic market, also in the high-end brand products niche.

The range of China's lead in merchandise exports is also getting wider, but it is narrower than the range of its lead in production: Some of the major products it makes are absorbed mostly by the domestic market. Also, growth of China's manufacturing industries creates a huge market for imported production inputs: parts, materials, and equipment, but Asia has been much more successful in tapping it than America and Europe.

For Western-based producers, China's emergence as the leader in global manufacturing and in merchandise exports leaves no other option but to search for niches to find a place in the new global division of labor. Our point is that U.S.-, Western Europe-, or Japan-based factories have no more opportunities in the low-end mass products segment—even if they use high technologies to make them. Their only chance is aggressive product differentiation, first of all in the high-end segment, preferably coupled with the development of export markets, especially the dynamic markets of China and other emerging world countries. The governments have to help.

Manufacturing activities in the West will be concentrating at a smaller number of factories deserving to be called excellent producers. Others, unfortunately, will have to either quit or clutch to a plank like a drowning man.

In contrast, analysis shows that the West has an excellent opportunity to sharpen its edge in services, especially those requiring high skills and special knowledge, and to drastically enhance their exports to China and other emerging countries whose services markets are still underdeveloped and where competitiveness of local service providers remains relatively low.

In the wake of globalization and the emergence of China as a new heavyweight, the Western world in general, and Western businesses in particular, has to look at the global economy from a new angle. It has to be viewed as really a single economic space, where every company from any Western country has to find the right position. If you choose to operate in your home country, you have to compile the list of competitive (in most cases, competitive means *globally* competitive) products (goods or services) you can produce there, and to stop producing anything else. If you choose to produce a particular kind of product, you have to find the place on the globe where you can make it with maximum efficiency. Those who are inflexible about both the product they make and the country they operate in—in other words, those not ready for the globalization era—will, most probably, fail.

Economic globalization in general, and competition from China in particular, lead to a new social differentiation in Western societies, threatening to erode their middle class.

As mentioned, facing strong competition from China, the West has only one really viable option: to aggressively differentiate products through higher quality, technological sophistication, exquisite design, branding, and so on. However, a large number of people (and, consequently, companies) in the West simply have no capacity or ability to succeed in the segment of differentiated high-end products, just as many people fail at the entrance exams to a first-rate university. The capacity-building problem in the West appears to be eventually as acute as in the developing world—the only difference is that here its gist is the development of high skills, not just acquisition of basic knowledge.

To those Western workers who are unprepared to produce products that require high skills, the verdict pronounced by the globalized economy is very tough: "Your compensation rates are too high as the same job can be done by other people at a much lower cost. Don't overestimate yourself!"

Those people who have high special skills and, above all, succeed in selling them—more and more often, the latter means getting a job in a first-rate globally oriented business organization, preferably engaged in some business with China or other emerging economies—feel fine, receiving increasingly high remuneration. In contrast, millions of other laborers, even those who received special training, are paid lower wages than they used to be, often have to work longer hours than in the past, and are hired only on a temporary basis to do the work that was previously done by regular employees. An example from real life: In Paris, a fashion designer trainee has to work six days a week from 9 A.M. to 9 P.M. for some 400 euros a month. And even if a young woman or man finds a regular job in the industry, she or he will be paid no more than 1,200 euros a month (is it possible to live for 1,200 euros a month in Paris?). All this resembles Chinese realities much more than established European employment standards. Perhaps some Chinese standards are starting to penetrate the Western world itself.

While China is rapidly enhancing its economic strength, most major Western economies are struggling with the aftershocks of the crisis of 2008–2009. In store for them is painful structural adjustment. Overall, with the end of the global economic boom of the mid-2000s all three major old centers of the world capitalist economy—the United States, many European countries, and Japan—entered a very difficult stage of their economic history.

For Japan, with the exception of a cohort of first-rate, mostly globally oriented companies, it is the time of sunset. Though not directly hit by the financial crisis of 2008–2009 like America and Europe, the country is rapidly losing its economic dynamism, vitality, and international importance. A worsening bias toward inefficient groupism in the management of companies and other organizations, a cult of mediocrity coupled with inability or a lack of will to promote leadership and talent, poor corporate governance, weak governments with messy economic policies, chronically low capacity to interact with the outer world, falling education standards—this is a short list of some major factors contributing to such an unfortunate state of affairs.

Major European economies are past their prime. Too much of too costly social protection, low work motivation, unsustainable welfare states, and disruptive social conflicts spurred by the attempts to scale them down, add to the structural problems the old continent has to fight to keep its economies going. Germany, though, appears to be a happy exception, along with a number of smaller countries like Switzerland, the Scandinavian states, or Luxembourg. On the other hand, the belt of vulnerable weak economies in the south and east of the continent is posing increasing economic, social, and political risks for Europe as a whole.

The United States has largely lost the dynamics of the 1990s, provided by the IT revolution and the high-tech entrepreneurship boom it spurred. In the 2000s, the U.S. economy became addicted to impetuous financial gambling, the financial sector absorbing too high a portion of the country's best brains. This financial drive joined by other Western economies ended in a disaster. Now it is still unclear what sectors and industries can generate the growth dynamics comparable to those created by the IT sector in the 1990s. Thus, currently the country remains in a growth vacuum.

However, the probability is high that the formation of the next cluster of key industries generating global growth will be prompted by the green revolution (renewable energy, smart grids, production of electric vehicles, and the like). We have shown that in these areas China is making quite an impressive start. The IT revolution was definitely led by the United States and carried out on the strength of its private, largely venture-style entrepreneurship. The green revolution will be different. The evidence is growing that this time a key to success will be close, large-scale, and productive interaction between the private sector and the state, and the outcome will decisively depend on the government's ability to exercise leadership and provide a set of incentives for both producers and consumers. In this regard, it may be China's turn to be in the vanguard.

To understand the essence of the West-China economic power shift, it is important to put it into the global context.

China's emergence as the first non-Western power center of the global capitalist economy reflects a shift in the world growth dynamics from the West to the emerging world, especially, in recent years, to large emerging economies. China is just one of them, though significantly exceeding all others in terms of both size and growth rates.

It will not emerge as a new world ruler either in the coming decades or in a more distant future. There will be no new Pax Sinica.

It will never establish a global position similar to the one Britain had in the nineteenth century and the United States—in the capitalist world—in the postwar decades until the 1970s (when its economic leadership began to be challenged by Japan) and then again—this time in the whole world—in the 1990s, after the demise of the Soviet Union and the start of Japan's fall as a great economic power. And no one else will. The epoch when the leadership of a single country was possible is over.

At its peak, U.S. dominance spread to effectively all areas, shaping the global power balance. It was the largest production power, trade power, technological power, financial power, and military power, as well as, of course, the most influential player in global politics.

In the new brave world of the early twenty-first century a single nation—be it America, China, or anyone else—is no longer capable of being a champion in all these areas across the board. The world is becoming more and more multipolar and, consequently, increasingly difficult to lead.

Multipolarization has its economic background.

In the 1960s–1980s, along with Japan, global growth was led by the small and medium-sized countries and territories of East Asia. In contrast, a very important feature of the global growth of the early twenty-first century is that large emerging economies around the world are joining the ranks of the fastest runners. Although no other large emerging countries can compare with China in terms of growth rates, not to mention size, their position in the global economy is also getting stronger, which enables them to raise their voices in international politics. Especially important is the increasing global influence of nations rich in natural resources.

Actually, the diplomacy of George W. Bush was a swan song of unilateralism. Its economic roots go back to America's IT rush of the 1990s, which made it, at that time, a single and unchallenged leader of the world economy. However, in the 2000s Bush's unilateralism caused an outcry around the globe. The world was already ripe for multilateralism.

A completely different diplomatic style, adopted by the Obama administration, manifests and confirms this global shift. Future Republican administrations will not set out on the Bush-style unilateralist path either—there is simply no way back.

But let us return to China. Along with the world's multipolarization, there are several other important reasons that are making its emergence as the only global leader effectively impossible.

The United States was and is the leader of the Western political and defense alliance. China, the largest country in the world, does not have any alliances around it. Actually, it doesn't have really important and strong political allies at all (dubious dictatorial, if not criminal, regimes it is consorting with don't count). Thus Beijing's steps aimed at boosting its global influence, especially when it tries to show its muscle, are counterbalanced through the teamwork of other nations whose interests are involved. Regional institutions like the ASEAN Forum, ASEAN Plus Three, and the East Asian Summits provide an institutional framework for such counterbalancing. The creation of the East Asian Community or a radical expansion of the Trans-Pacific Partnership can strengthen it further.

Next, with its domestic development problems and potentially explosive social tensions, especially those due to its unique size, China is destined to be much more inward-oriented than Britain of the nineteenth century and America of the second half of the twentieth century. Among other things, it is difficult to imagine it as the major provider of international public goods, especially in the vital, though often thankless role of the global policeman.

Also, for China it will be much more difficult if not impossible to develop global soft power—a necessary prerequisite for global leadership—comparable to that of the United States. American economic, social and political models, values, way of life, mentality, and mass culture have found great numbers of supporters and admirers all around the world. In China's case it will not be so—both because Chinese characters are more difficult to remember than English letters and because the Chinese model as such simply does not have the attractiveness needed to find the way to the hearts of many people on the planet. Actually, China does not seem to be even thinking about this sort of influence, insisting only on other countries' noninterference into its internal affairs.

No, China won't be the world's ruler or the only world leader.

It is, however, taking the lead in a number of crucially important areas. The West retains and may increase its advantages in others. It is possible that new fast runners among large emerging economies will, little by little, also find niches where they can be number one. India is already leading in exports of software and related services. Even in the long term, China will hardly outperform the West in technologies, branding, and ability to provide high quality goods and services. The maximum it can achieve in these areas is to become an equal competitor.

Beyond the economy, the United States and the West as a whole have and, at least for the foreseeable future, will retain a much stronger military power and a bigger say on international security issues. Unlike the economic field, China's role in addressing key international security issues outside Asia remains limited and mostly symbolic.

To summarize, the West-China economic power shift does not mean that the West is or will be conceding to China the role of the global leader. Not at all.

This shift is the core of the process of the world's multipolarization.

Let us finish on an optimistic note—optimistic especially for the Western side.

The contours of a new world are taking shape: a world that is not West-centered and whose major economic dynamics, in terms of the increase of production, consumption, trade, investment, and so on, are coming mostly from outside the West. However, this dynamism of non-Western nations, China first and foremost, has a good side for the West as well.

For Westerners, a rapidly growing China opens an array of new opportunities. To take advantage of them, and also to know the challenger better, Westerners have to learn much more about China. Schools and universities in America, Europe, and Japan must offer more Chinese language courses as well as courses on the Chinese history, culture, economy, and politics. Business schools have to teach Chinese business. There should be many more translations of Chinese books: classical and contemporary literature, books on business, economy, politics, history, and so on. All this can provide impetus for many more people to discover their China opportunities.

Opportunity is there—move and try to find it. It can be a business, a job, or at least a very valuable experience.

Try to discover your China. Study the language if you have some spare time. Read. Watch videos. Take a journey. Walk slowly through the Forbidden City and feel the astounding greatness of the Great Wall of China, but don't limit your stay to Beijing and Shanghai. Go to the hinterland. Remember the names and locations of all the provinces. Talk to people. Try to understand the national character, mentality, culture.

If you are a businessman, try to establish business channels to find your market niche and perhaps an opportunity to produce or to invest. If you are an expert in a particular field, you may find a good China job. The number of Westerners working for Chinese firms and other organizations, still not that large, is increasing, slowly but surely, and the pace of the increase will accelerate. If you are a civil servant working for the central or local government in your country, explore China to get important hints about the ways to give the economy of your country or locality new energy.

Make China part of your world. Even if it does not lead to a good business opportunity, you will gain knowledge and experience that may help you a great deal to live and work in today's new world. And if your opportunity works out really well, you will join the ranks of Western beneficiaries of China's growth.

For Western businessmen, there is also another way around to benefit from the Chinese challenge. To do well in a global economy where China is a leading player, you can leverage your national identity and tradition, emphasizing complete non-Chineseness. Make a sales point out of the fact that you have nothing to do with China: You don't have factories there; you don't outsource; you offer something entirely different, which is beyond China's reach. Like a high-end Nisshin food store in Tokyo where the paper on the notice board proudly informs customers that the store sells absolutely nothing from China. Or like producers of Swiss watches, Italian tile, Bohemian glass, German precision devices, and so on.

After all, in China they make a wide range of products en masse, while every single item you produce at home is a state-of-the-art piece, a symbol of quality and high taste, a product of your nonstop race toward perfection.

Isn't it?

References

ADB. 2011. "Key Indicators for Asia and the Pacific 2010." Manila: Asian Development Bank. www.adb.org/Documents/Books/Key_Indicators/2010/pdf/PRC.pdf/. ·

AFP. 2010. "French Budget Makes 'Historic' Spending Cuts." www.breitbart.com/article.php?id=CNG.5fd9d9aca2e24cbdb73350eb1197d306.7b1&show_article=1/.

Alexander, Philippe. 2011. "Europe Lags US Securitization Revival." *The Banker*, February 18. www.thebanker.com/Markets/Capital-Mkts/Europe-lags-US-securitization-revival?utm-campaign=March%20e-newsletter%202&utm-source=emailCampaign&utm-medium=email/.

Amronin, Gene, and Anna Paulson. 2009. "Comparing Patterns of Default Among Prime and Subprime Mortgages." *Economic Perspectives* 33 (2): 18–37.

An, Emma. 2011. "Overseas Acquisitions by Chinese Companies Offer Rewards and Risks," *China Daily* (HK Edition). January 14, www.chinadaily.com.cn/hkedition/2011-01/14/content_11850205.htm/.

Anderson, Curt, 2010. "Wachovia to Settle Drug-Money Laundering Case." AP, March 17. www.msnbc.msn.com/id/35914759/ns/business-world_business/.

AP. 2010. "UK Plans Toughest Austerity Program Since WWII." www.telegram.com/article/20101020/NEWS/101029993/1052/rss01&source=rss/.

APCO Worldwide. 2010. "China's 12th Five-Year Plan." http://apcoworldwide.net/content/PDFs/Chinas_12th_Five_Year_Plan.pdf/.

Asia Society's Center on U.S.-China Relations, Pew Center on Global Climate Change. 2009. "A Roadmap for U.S.-China Cooperation on Energy and Climate Change." www.pewclimate.org./docUploads/US-China-Roadmap-Feb2009.pdf/.

Atkinson, James. 2011. "Huawei Launches Android-Powered IDEOS X5 Smartphone." *Mobile Magazine*, January 6. www.mobiletoday.co.uk/News/10849/huawei_launches_Android_powered_ideos_x5_smartphone.aspx/.

Beijing Review. 2009. "Powering the Future." October 29. www.bjreview.com.cn/quotes/xt/2009-10/26/content_225645.htm/.

Biggs, Stuart. 2010. "Rutgers' Chinese Solar Panels Show Clean-Energy Shift." Bloomberg, July 23. www.bloomberg.com/news/2010-07-22/rutgers-chinese-connection-signals-solar-panels-coming-to-roof-near-you.html/.

Brautigam, Deborah. 2010. "Africa's Eastern Promise," *Foreign Affairs*, January 5. www.foreignaffairs.com/articles/65916/deborah-brautigam/africa%E2%80%899s-eastern-promise/.

Bundesbank. 2010. "German Balance of Payments in 2009." www.bundesbank.de/download/volkswirtschaft/mba/2010/201033mba-en-german.pdf/.

Bundesbank. 2011. "Germany's International Investment Position." www.bundesbank.de/download/statistik/sdds/stat-auslandsvermoegen/sdds_auslandsvermoegen_quartal.en.pdf/.

Bureau of Economic Analysis. 2011a. "National Economic Accounts." www.bea.gov/national/.

Bureau of Economic Analysis. 2011b. "International Economic Accounts." www.bea.gov/international/.

Cheng Hui-yuan. 2011. "New 5-Year Plan for China's Auto Industry May Be Scrapped." *Want China Times*, May 12. www.wantchinatimes.com/news-subclass-cnt.aspx?&cid=1102&MainCatID=20110512000014.

Chiiki Kasseika Jyanaru. 2011. "Chiiki Kigyo-o Kasseika saseru Niigata-ken to Kita-Kanto-to-no Sangyo Renkei-o Kangaeru. Kanagata Sangyo-o Jirei-to shite." March. Kamo City, Niigata.

China Daily. 2006. "Huawei Wins First Major German Deal." November 16. http://english.people.com.cn/200611/16/eng20061116_322001.html/.

China Daily. 2011. "China Beats Emission Reduction Target." January 14, www.chinadaily.com.cn/photo/2011-01/14/content_11856791.htm/.

China Post. 2011. "Foreign Direct Investment Growth to Remain Robust: Commerce Ministry." February 21. www.chinapost.com.tw/business/asia-china/2011/02/21/291803/Foreign-direct.htm/.

Chung, Olivia. 2007. "Carlyle Saga Puts Spotlight on China Takeovers." Asia Times Online. www.atimes.com/atimes/China_Business/IC24Cb02.html/.

Copeland, Michael. 2006. "The Mighty Micro-Multinational," *Business 2.0*, July 1. money.cnn.com/magazines/business2/business2-archive/2006/07/01/8380230/index.htm/.

DHMQ. 2010. "Furniture Industry in China: Invest in China." DHMQ Business&Investment Service, April 14. www.Chinesebusinessservice.com/dailyfresh/221.html/.

DIR. 2010. "Chugoku-ni Okeru Kojin Kinyu Shisan 5 Cho Doru-o Koeteiru." Asian Insight, www.dir.co.jp/souken/asian/asian-insight/101215.html/.

Dyer, Geoff, Jamil Anderlin, and Henry Sender. 2011. "China Lending Hits New Heights." FT.com, January 17. www.ft.com/cms/5/0/488c60f4-2281-11eO-b6a2-00144feab49a.html/.

EC Commission. 2011. "Trade: China." http://ec.europa.eu.en/trade/creating-opportunities/bilateral-relations/countries/china/.

Farrell Diana, Ulrich Gersch, and Elizabeth Stephenson. 2006. "The Value of China's Emerging Middle Class." *McKinsey Quarterly*, June. https://www.mckinseyquaterly.com/Marketing/Sectors_Regions?The_value_of_Chinas_emerging_middle_class_1798/.

Feldstein, Martin. 2009. "America's Saving Rate and the Dollar Future." Project Syndicate, July, https//www.uber.org/Feldstein/projectsyndicate072009.pdf.

Fernandez, Juan, Per Jenster, and Robert Loane. 2011. "2nd Annual CEIBS Foreign Executives in China Survey." January 6. www.ceibs.edu/knowledge/papers/58192.shtml/.

Gandel, Stephen. 2011. "After Three Years and Trillions of Dollars, Our Banks Still Don't Work." *Daily Yomiuri*, September 24 (Reprinted from *Time* magazine).

Glick, Reuven, and Kevin Lansing. 2010. "Global Household Leverage, House Prices, and Consumption." Federal Reserve Bank of San Francisco, January 11. www.frbsf.org/publications/economics/letter/2010/el2010-01.html/.

Global Finance. 2011. "Household Saving Rates." www.gfmag.com/tools/global-database-economic-data/10396-household-saving-rates.html#axzz1IwQEiLzc/.

Gogoi, Pallavi. 2011. "Government Will Begin Selling AIG Stock." www.dispatch.com/live/content/national-world/stories/2011/01/15/government-will-begin-selling-its-aig-stock.html/.

Govt Vacancies. 2010. "Life Insurance Corporation of India, LIC." www.govtvacancies.com/life-insurance-corporation-of-india-lic.html/.

Griffin, Peter. 2007. "China's Technological Challenger." *NZ Herald*, March 15. www.nzherald.co.nz/telecomminications/news/article.cfm?&-id=93&object=10428813/.

Harris, Dan. 2010. "Which Comes First: The Wealth or the Low End?" China Law Blog, www.chinalawblog.com/2009/04/foreign_companies_going_china .html/.

Higgins, Andrew. 2011. "From China, an End Run Around U.S. Tariffs." *Washington Post:* A Special Report for *Yomiuri Shimbun. Daily Yomiuri,* May 28.

Howes, Stephen. 2010. "China's Energy Intensity Target: On-Track or Off." East Asia Forum. www.eastasiaforum.org/2010/03/31/chinas-energy-intensity-target-on-track-or-off/.

IMF. 2009a. "Global Financial Stability Report." April. www.imf.org/external/ pubs/ft/gfsr/2009/01/pdf/chap.1.pdf/.

IMF. 2009b. "Global Financial Stability Report." October. www.imf.org/ external/pubs/ft/gfsr/2009/02/pdf/chap.1.pdf/.

IMF. 2011. "World Economic Outlook Database." September. www.imf.org/ external/pubs/ft/weo/2011/02/weodata/index.aspx/.

Institute of Chinese Affairs. 2006. "Chugoku Nenkan 2006." Tokyo: Soshisha.

Institute of Chinese Affairs. 2011. "Chugoku Nenkan 2011." Tokyo: Mainichi Shimbunsha.

Insurance Regulatory and Development Authority. 2011. "Report of the Committee on Bank Assurance." www.bimabazaar.com/contents/BANKASSURANCE% 20REPORT.pdf/.

Insurancereview. 2009. "General Cover Premium to Top Rs 1 Lakh Cr by 2015." www.insurancereview.in/posts/list/articles-general-cover-premium-to-top-rs-1-lakh-cr-by-2015-910096.htm/.

International Steel Statistics Bureau. 2011. "Global Overview." www.issb.co.uk/ global.html/.

Jin, Jianmin. 2010. "Foreign Companies Accelerating R&D Activity in China." Fujitsu Research Institute, May 13. http://jp.fujitsu.com/group/fri/en/ column/message/2010/2010-05-13.html/.

Jones, Marie 2010. "Haier Tops Global Appliances Rankings Again." Channelnews, December 13. www.channelnews.com.au/Appliances? KitchenW7A8M4N9/.

Knowledge & Wharton. 2006. "The Long and Winding Road to Privatization in China." May 10. http://knowledge.wharton.upenn.edu/article.cfm?articleid= 1472/.

Koopman Robert, Wang Zhi, and Wei Shang Jin. 2009. "How Much of Chinese Exports Is Really Made in China?" World Bank. http://siteresources .worldbank.org/INTRANETTRADE/Resources/Internal-Training/ 287823-1256848879189/6526508-1283456658475/7370147-1308070299728/ 7997263-1308070314933/PAPER_10_Koopman_Wang.pdf/.

KPMG. 2010. "Mainland China Banking Survey 2010." www.kpmg.de/docs/China-banking-survey-2010-_2010008.pdf/.

Kujis Louis, and Gao Xu. 2008. "China's Fiscal Policy—Moving to Center Stage." Stanford Center for International Development conference. October. http://scid.stanford.edu/group/siepr/cgi-bin/scid/?q=system/files/shared/kuijs_10-16-08.pdf/.

Levesque, Tylene. 2007. "Rizhao: China's Solar-Powered Sunshine City." *Inhabitat.* http://inhabitat.com/rizhao-the sunshine-city/.

Loveday, Eric. 2010. "China's Electric Vehicle Production Could Reach One Million by 2020." *Autobloggreen,* http://green.autoblog.com//201o/10/19/chinas-electric-vehicle-production-could-reach-one-million-by-2/.

Lum Thomas, Hannah Fischer, Julissa Gomes-Granger, and Anne Leland. 2009. "China's Foreign Aid Activities in Africa, Latin America and Southeast Asia." Congressional Research Service, February. www.fas.org/sgp/crs/row/R40361.pdf/.

Maeda, Seiji. 2007. "China's Environmental and Energy Problems and the Possibility of Japan-China Technical Cooperation." www.nistep.go.jp/achiev/ftxeng/stfc/stt022e/qr22pdf/STTqr2205.pdf/.

Market Research. 2011. "China Insurance Sector Analysis." http://businesreserc.worldpress.com/2011/03/25/china-insurance-sector-analysis/.

Maruyama, Junichi. 2010. "Clutching at Straws Not Always Doom and Gloom." *Daily Yomiuri,* May 19.

McKinsey. 2006. "China's High-Tech Market: A Race to the Middle." *McKinsey Quarterly.* https://www.mckinseyquarterly.com/High_Tech/Hardware?China's_high_tech_market_a_race_to_the_middle_1854/.

McKinsey. 2007. "Governing China's Boards: An Interview with John Thornton." *McKinsey Quaterly,* February. www.mkkinseyquaterly.com/strategy/Globalization/Governing-Chinas-boards-An-interview-with-John-Thornton-1920/.

McKinsey. 2009a. "The Coming of Age. China's New Class of Wealthy Consumers." *Insights China.* www.mckinsey.com/locations/greaterchina/mckonchina/reports/mckinsey_wealthy_consumer_report.pdf/.

McKinsey. 2009b. "McKinsey: China Needs to Promote Long-Term Savings and Production Functions of Life Insurance Industry." www.mckinsey.com/locations/greaterchina/mckonchina/reports/china_life_insurance_industry.aspx/.

Menoir Casa. 2011. "About Brand." http://menoir.ciffol/menoir/brand_en.shtml/.

METI. 2010. "Results of the Fifth Japan-China Energy Conservation Forum." www.meti.go.jp/english/press/data/20101025_01.html/.

Ministry of Finance Japan. 2011. "International Investment Position of Japan." www.mof.go.jp/english/international_policy/reference/iip/e2010.htm/.

Ministry of Internal Affairs and Communications. 2011. "Japan Statistical Yearbook 2011." www.stat.go.jp/english/data/nenkan/index.htm/.

National Bureau of Statistics. 2010. "China Statistical Yearbook 2009." Beijing.

Nikkei. 2011a. "Chugoku, Baibai 27-bai-ni Kyudzo," *Nikkei Shimbun,* March 3.

Nikkei. 2011b. "Oshugin, Hongyo Shudo de Kaifuku," *Nikkei Shimbun,* March 3.

Nikkei. 2011c. "Bei Kinyu, Shueki Kaizen," *Nikkei Shimbun,* January 22.

Nikkei. 2011d. "Chugoku, Furyo Saiken 5500 Oku Yen," *Nikkei Shimbun,* March 30.

Norris, Teryn. 2010. "Watch: China Building Ambitious 'Solar Valley City' to Advance Solar Industry." http://itsgettinghothere.org/2010/04/18/watch-china-building-ambitious-solar-valley-city-to-advance-solar-industry/.

OECD. 2010. "OECD Factbook 2010." www.oecd-ilibrary.org/economics/oecd-factbook-2010_factbook-2010-en/.

OECD. 2011. "Economic Outlook No 89." June. http://stats.oecd.org/Index.aspx?QueryId=29790/.

Oerlikon. 2010. "The Fiber Year 2009/10. A World Survey on Textiles and Nonwovens Industry." www.oerlikon.com/ecomaXL/get_blob.php?name=The_Fiber_Year_2010_en_0607_[1].pdf/.

Partlow, Joshua. 2009. "Afghan Minister Accused of Taking Bribe." *Washington Post,* November 17. www.washingtonpost.com/wp-dyn/content/article/2009111704198.html/.

Peel, Quentin. 2010. "Merkel Spells Out 80 bn Euro Spending Cuts." FT.com, June 7. www.ft.com/intl/cms/s/0/of9548c8-7256-11df-9f82-00144feabdc0.html#axzzIOYrj4cnw/.

Powell, Bill. 2011. "The End of Cheap Labor in China." *Time,* June 27; *Daily Yomiuri,* June 28.

Redding, Gordon, and Michael Witt. 2009. "The Future of Chinese Capitalism: Choices and Chances." Oxford University Press.

Red-Luxury.com. 2010. "High-End Furniture Makers Target China." http://red-luxury.com/2010/08/04/high-end-furniture-makers-target-china/.

Rein, Shaun. 2010. "Chinese Companies Can't Build Brands?" *Bloomberg BusinessWeek,* January 26. www.businessweek.com/globally/content/jan2010/gb20100126_512186htm/.

ResearchInChina. 2010. "China Textile and Apparel Production and Sales Statistics 2009." www.researchinchina.com/Htmls/Report/2010/5843.html/.

Reuter. 2011. "China Says Has Helped Europe by Buying Debt." http://finance.yahoo.com/news/China-says-has-helped-Europe-rb-550120513.html?x=0/.

RIETI. 2010. "RIETI-TID 2010." Tokyo: Research Institute of Economy, Trade & Industry. www.rieti-tid.com/.

Roth, Zachary. 2011. "Key from the Speech: What's in Obama's Deficit Reduction Plan?" Yahoo! News, April 13. http://news.yahoo.com/s/yblog-thelookout/20110413/ts_yblog_thelookout/key-from-the-speech-whats-in-obamas-deficit-reduction-plan/.

Schneider, Howard. 2011. "Beijing Blues: How to Handle All Those Trillion of Dollars." *Yomiuri Daily*, April 22. Washington Post Special Report.

Searchina. 2011. "2010Nen Jiten-de Chugoku-no Taigai Kinyu Shisangaku ga 4 Cho 1260 Oku Doru." http://headlines.yahoo.co.jp/he?a=20110530-00000064-scn-cn/.

Shintaku, Seita. 2010. "Sangyozai-no Kyosoryoku-ga Kagi." *Nikkei* (October 1): 33.

Simpson Thatcher & Barlett. 2011. "Private Equity 2011." www.stblaw.com/content/publications/pub1221.pdf/.

Taniguchi Masatsugu. 2009. "Afugan-de Beikoku wa Senso, Chugoku wa Do:Ko:zan-no Shutoku." http://business.nikkeibp.co.jp/article/manage/20091214/211568/.

Trading Economics. 2010. "Euro Area GDP Rises by 0.3% in Q4." www.tradingeconomics.com/Economics/GDP-Growth:aspx?Symbol=EURO/.

Treanor, Gill. 2008. "Toxic Shock: How the Banking Industry Created a Global Crisis." *Guardian*, April 8. www.guardian.co.uk/business/2008/apr/08/creditcrunch.banking/.

Truman, Edwin. 2010. "The Management of China's International Reserves and Its Sovereign Wealth Funds." Peterson Institute for International Economics. www.iie.com/publications/papers/paper/cfm?ResearchID=1074/.

Tselichtchev, Ivan, 2010. "Chinese Takeaway." *Business Outlook*, June 12. www.business.outlookindia.com/article.aspx?265707/.

Tselichtchev, Ivan, and Philippe Debroux. 2009. "Asia's Turning Point." Singapore: John Wiley & Sons.

Tsuchiya, Takayasu. 2010. "Chugoku-no Enerugi Shigen Seisaku." www.ndl.go.jp/data/publication/document/2011/201002_09.pdf/.

21 Seiki Chugoku Soken. 2006. *Chugoku Joho Handobukku 2006 Nenban*. Tokyo: Sososha.

21 Seiki Chugoku Soken. 2010. *Chugoku Joho Handobukku 2010 Nenban*. Tokyo: Sososha.

21 Seiki Chugoku Soken. 2011. *Chugoku Joho Handobukku 2011 Nenban*. Tokyo: Sososha.

UN. 2010. "National Account Main Aggregates Data Base." http://unstats.un.org/unsd/snaama/dnllist.asp/.

UNIDO. 2011. "International Yearbook of Industrial Statistics." Northampton, MA: Edward Elgar Publishing.

U.S. Census Bureau. 2011a. "Statistical Abstract of the United States 2011." www.census.gov/compendia/statab/.

U.S. Census Bureau. 2011b. "Trade in Goods with China." www.census.gov/foreign-trade/balance/c5700.html#2010.

U.S. Chamber of Commerce. 2010. "China's Drive for Indigenous Innovation." www.uschamber.com/sites/default/files/reports/100728chinareport_0.pdf/.

Wang, Xin, and Yi Wen. 2011. "Can Rising Housing Prices Explain China's High Household Saving Rate?" *Federal Reserve Bank of St. Louis Review*, March 2011. http://research.stlouisfed.org/publications/review/11/03/67-88Wang.pdf/.

Wang, Xing. 2008. "Huawei, Global Marine Systems in Telecom JV." *China Daily*, December 18. www.chinadaily.com.cn/bizchina/2008-12/18/content-7319164.htm/.

Want China Times. 2011. "Electric Vehicles Are Key to China's Future: Study." April 21. www.wantchinatimes.com/news-subclass-cnt.aspx?cid=1205&MainCatID=12&id=20110421000091/.

Weagley, Robert. 2010. "One Big Difference Between Chinese and American Households: Debt." http://blogs.forbes.com/moneybuilder/2010/06/24/one-big-difference-between-chinese-and-american-househplds-debt/.

Westaway, Luke. 2011. "Huawei Ideos X5 and Ideos X6 Review: Hands-on with Two New Android Smartphones." Cnet.uk. http://crave.cnet.co.uk/mobiles/huawei-ideos-x5-and-ideos-x6-review-hands-on-with-two-new-android-smartphones-500021535/.

Williamson, Peter. 2004. "'Buying the Brand': China's Shortcut to World Markets." Asia Today Online, February 16. www.asiatoday.comau/feature_reports.php?id=158/.

Willis, Bob. 2011. "U.S. Economy: Growth Accelerates on Consumer Spending." Bloomberg, January 29, www.bloomberg.com/news/2011-01-28/u-s-economy-expands-amid-biggest-gain-in-consumer-spending-in-four-years.html.

Winter, Michael. 2010. "Wachovia Helped Launder Mexican Drug Money." *USA Today*, June 29. http://content.usatoday.com/communities/ondeadline/post/2010/06/reyiport-wachovia-bank-helped-launder-mexican-drug-money/1/.

World Bank. 2011. "World Development Indicators."

World Steel Association. 2010. "Steel Statistical Yearbook 2010." www.worldsteel.org/picture/publicationfiles/SSY%202010.pdf/.

WTO. 2010. International Trade Statistics 2002, 2008–2010. www.wto.org/english/res_e/statis_e/its09-world_trade_dev_e.htm/.

WTO. 2011. "International Trade and Tariff Data." www.wto.org./english/res_e/statis_e?statis_e.htm.

Xia, Olive. 2011. "China Insurance Sector." Core Pacific—Yamaichi. www.cpy.com/hk/CPY/research/pdf/2011Q1_en/2011_insurance.pdf/.

Xinhua. 2007. "China, Japan Enhance Ties in Energy, Environment." www.chinadaily.com.cn/china/2007-09/27/content_6140161.htm/.

Xinhua. 2011. "China Sets Long-Term Timetable to Guide Pollution Fight." http://news.xinhuanet.com/english2010/china/2011-04/21/c_13840/46.htm/.

Yano Tsuneta Kinenkai. 2011. "Sekai Kokusei Dzue 2010/2011." Tokyo.

About the Author

Ivan Tselichtchev, currently professor at the Niigata University of Management, Japan, is an internationally renowned expert and writer on the global and Asian economy and business—actively writing in English, Japanese, and Russian. He is the author of four books, the co-author of the recent popular book, *Asia's Turning Point* (John Wiley & Sons, 2009), a contributor to many other academic publications, and the author of around 200 articles.

Ivan Tselichtchev was born in 1956 in Moscow, USSR; graduated from Moscow University in 1979, joining Russia's leading think tank the Institute of World Economy and International Relations the same year; got his PhD in Economics in 1983; and became a Senior Fellow in 1984. In 1989, he came to Japan as the Institute's representative and also as the Guest Researcher at the Japan Center for Economic Research in Tokyo. Teaching in Niigata since 1994, he has also worked as a part-time faculty member in a number of leading universities in Japan and lectured in different countries around the world. He is a commentator for the CNBC international TV network. In Gorbachev's *perestroika* years, he was awarded the Labor Valor Medal. In 2004, the Cabinet Office of the Government of Japan named Ivan Tselichtchev Seikatsu Tatsujin (A Master of Life), which means a person with outstanding achievements and lifestyle.

221

Index